"Words can't express how thankful I am for this curriculum teacher, I know how impossible it is to find truly gospel-c(that young people can process . . . and will find interestin culture awash with moralistic messages and frilly silliness news written for young minds. Seriously, I can't recomm

Elyse Fitzpatrick, Author of *Good News for Weary Women* и ...

"What an amazing gift, *What's Up?* is going to be for middle-school and junior-high ministry, and parents of fifth through eighth-graders. Debbie Harrell and Jack Klumpenhower have done an outstanding job of contextualizing the gospel of God's grace for kids in one of the most vulnerable and formative seasons of life. I get excited just thinking about how this curriculum, in the hands of grace-loving leaders, will help disciple a new generation of gospel-equipped, Jesus-loving students. And let me add, the teachers are going to benefit just as much as the students. Great job, Debbie and Jack. More, more, more!"

Dr. Scotty Ward Smith, Founding Pastor of Christ Community Church; Teacher in Residence at West End Community Church; author of *Everyday Prayers: 365 Days to a Gospel-Centered Faith*

"Have you ever wondered how you could explain the great truths of the gospel to your children? *What's Up?* takes you step by step with solid teaching, thoughtful questions, insights, and practical application—always leading you to Christ. It is a must-read for parents, teachers, young and old."

Rose Marie Miller, Author of *From Fear to Freedom* and *Nothing Is Impossible with God*

"If you read Jack Klumpenhower's book, *Show Them Jesus*, but didn't think you could teach as well as Jack does—don't worry. The *What's Up?* curriculum and teacher's guide give you everything you need to teach your middle school students the same amazing gospel lessons Jack presented in his book. You'll have parents thanking you for the amazing way their kids are learning deep gospel truths like justification, adoption, how to recognize false repentance, and how to offer true forgiveness. It doesn't matter what curriculum you are currently using with your middle school, put it on hold and get your kids through this material—that is what I am going to do at my church."

Marty Machowski, Family Life Pastor and author of *Long Story Short* and *Old Story New*, *The Gospel Story Bible*, the *Gospel Story for Kids* curriculum and *Prepare Him Room*

"Preteens can be critics. It's just part of how we grow at that age. Deborah and Jack know the best way to fight a critical spirit—a clear vision of Jesus, an honest assessment of our hearts, and a faithful commitment to working out the implications of the gospel in our relationships. *What's Up?* is a clear and engaging tool for applying these truths to middle school kids."

Jared Kennedy, Pastor of Families, Sojourn Community Church, Louisville, KY

"I love this study! Deborah Harrell and Jack Klumpenhower have done a fine job at communicating gospel-saturated truth for students and have given teachers a reliable and easy-to-use guide. *What's Up?* is a helpful tool to faithfully plant and water the gospel of Jesus Christ in the hearts of students. If you are looking for a biblical, Christ-centered, and holistic study for teenagers, look no further!"

Brian H. Cosby, Author of *Giving Up Gimmicks: Reclaiming Youth Ministry from an Entertainment Culture* and *Rebels Rescued: A Student's Guide to Reformed Theology*; pastor and visiting professor at Reformed Theological Seminary

"Congratulations to Deborah and Jack for taking on the most challenging group of all—our kids. In *What's Up?* they attempt to teach young people both the gospel and how to live out of the gospel. Why wait until we get locked into a pattern of performing or pretending? Why not be discipled in the gospel from the beginning? That is what these creative and engaging lessons do and do well."

Stephen Smallman, Assistant Pastor, New Life Presbyterian Church, Glenside, PA; author of *The Walk-Steps for New and Renewed Followers of Jesus*

"Harrell and Klumpenhower's *What's Up?* middle school curriculum beautifully lives up to its subtitle: *Discovering the Gospel, Jesus, and Who You REALLY Are*. I love its thoroughness, flexibility, and teaching style. More importantly, its model of student discipleship (believe—don't just try harder) coupled with the practical 'make-it-stick' section packs a powerful gospel-driven one-two punch. It should be required curriculum for all youth ministries!"

John C. Kwasny, PhD, Director, *One Story Ministries*

"*What's Up?* is a curriculum that will challenge both students and teachers to delve deep into the definition, meaning, and significance of Christianity. It encourages students to look squarely into their hearts and discover whether or not they are truly living for themselves or for their Creator."

Susan Wall, Children's Ministry Curriculum Coordinator, Capitol Hill Baptist Church, Washington, DC

WHAT'S UP?

Discovering the Gospel, Jesus, and Who You REALLY Are

Deborah Harrell and Jack Klumpenhower

New Growth Press

WWW.NEWGROWTHPRESS.COM

What's Up? Discovering the Gospel, Jesus, and Who You REALLY Are (Teacher Guide)

New Growth Press, Greensboro, NC 27404

These lessons are based on the large body of teaching material developed by Serge, especially the lessons contained in the *Sonship* (1988) and *Gospel Transformation* (2001, 2006) courses. Readers familiar with those materials will find many of the concepts and illustrations contained in them repeated in these lessons. In particular, Lessons 2, 7, 11, and 12 in this book are greatly influenced by Lessons 1, 7, 12, and 19 of *Gospel Transformation*. The report card illustration used in Lesson 4 is based on similar Serge illustrations and first appeared in an unpublished curriculum, *Blessed to Be a Blessing* by Jack Klumpenhower, 2007.

Cover and Interior designed by Matthew Bomberger
ISBN 978-1-939946-81-2

Printed in the United States of America

22 21 20 19 18 17 16 15   2 3 4 5 6

TABLE OF CONTENTS

UNIT ONE: THE GOSPEL

UNIT TWO: YOUR HEART

UNIT THREE: A CHANGED LIFE

TEACHER'S INTRODUCTION

Welcome to *What's Up? Discovering the Gospel, Jesus, and Who You Really Are*! This study introduces the gospel to Middle School (5th–8th grade) students, and helps those who believe it to live out that good news of Jesus.

The gospel says believers are joined to Jesus. *He* is their identity. Young people who know this good news are confident and secure in him. They aren't batted around by the praises and put-downs bombarding them from the outside. They're renewed *from the inside*.

As a *What's Up?* leader, you have the opportunity to be part of that process. Your job is to help your students see Jesus. You'll encourage them to believe his gospel—at the heart level. You'll show them how being joined to him breaks down those outside pressures they feel. You'll help them connect the gospel to daily life.

WHO IS THIS STUDY FOR?

Because *What's Up?* is about believing and living out the gospel, it's good for both students who aren't yet believers and believers of all maturity levels. A basic knowledge of the Bible is helpful and the lessons assume that most students will have this. Yet the lessons also define key terms and provide background information in order to help students who may not have had much Bible exposure or are exploring Christianity.

- Unbelievers will learn about Jesus, the salvation he offers, and his call to believe the gospel. They'll also get a look at what many gospel presentations to unbelievers miss: how believing leads to huge changes in how they live and relate to God and others. They'll be prepared to choose Jesus with an understanding that the gospel is not only a way to be forgiven, but also a transforming truth to live out.

- Believers will develop a deeper appreciation for the gospel and how to apply it daily to their lives. They'll be challenged to believe *more fully*. Don't be surprised if students who've professed faith for years tell you that the course is giving them new, deeper insight into the condition of their hearts, all Jesus has done for them, and the implications of living out the gospel.

What's Up? is designed for group study. Sharing with others is an important part of the learning process, so the lessons will be most helpful if students have others to work and learn alongside of them. A student can do the study alone, but in that case *your* role as leader and mentor becomes even more important. You'll need to be prepared to do every part of the study with the student and to share experiences with the material even more than you ordinarily would with a group.

WHAT SUPPLIES ARE NEEDED?

Each student will need:

- **Student Guide.** Students should be reminded to take home their copy of the *Student Guide* each week to complete the Make It Stick assignments and bring them back to class the following week for discussion.

- **Bible.** The lessons mostly use the English Standard Version (ESV) Bible.

- **Pen or pencil.**

Most importantly, *What's Up?* is committed to the "supplies" the *Holy Spirit* provides. These are less tangible than the lesson pages and pencils, but you'll find them to be the guiding principles behind the approach to all the lessons. These supplies from the Spirit are:

1. The Word of God. The Holy Spirit speaks through the Bible. These lessons will use the Bible to teach and will get students reading the Bible.

2. Prayer. The Holy Spirit helps believers pray. The lessons and assignments in *What's Up?* will include lots of prayer.

3. The good news of Jesus. Jesus and his cross are the central message of God's Word, and the Holy Spirit loves to tell about Jesus. These lessons will keep calling students to believe in Jesus and all the blessings that come through him.

4. Other believers. The Holy Spirit makes believers part of God's family. These lessons get students sharing with a group, talking about their faith with others, and learning from you, their leader and mentor.

HOW IS THE COURSE ORGANIZED?

What's Up? comprises fifteen lessons that are grouped around three themes or units.

UNIT ONE: THE GOSPEL

Lessons 1 through 5 explain the good news of Jesus. They cover sin and its effects, the person who saves us from sin, and the key aspects of that salvation.

LESSON 1: OH . . . *NOW* I SEE

Big Idea: Seeing Jesus

Everyone has an idea of who God is and what it means to be a Christian. This first lesson looks at some of the "blurry" ideas we can have about believing in Jesus, and replaces them with the clear truth about the who, what, how, and why of the gospel.

LESSON 2: THAT'S MY WHOLE LIFE STORY

Big Idea: The Gospel Story

The gospel takes place within the story of creation, fall, and redemption in Jesus. It's easy to think big parts of this story don't directly involve us, but this lesson shows how every believer in Jesus has been a part of the story right from the start—and will be forever.

LESSON 3: MY TONGUE IS CONNECTED TO MY—WHAT?

Big Idea: Sin of the Heart

The things we say reveal that our outward sin bubbles up from deep in our hearts. This lesson reveals how we tend to want to prove ourselves right, but can't earn our salvation by being good enough for God. We need a change only Jesus can give.

LESSON 4: HMM . . . WHAT GRADES DO I GET?

Big Idea: Justification by Faith

If we think we can make ourselves "right" by the things we say or do, we're fooling ourselves. Only the righteousness God gives in Jesus can ever make us right in his eyes. This lesson shows how we get this by faith in Jesus; a faith that deepens throughout our lives.

LESSON 5: PRESENTS? FOR ME?!

Big Idea: Holiness and Fighting Sin

This lesson teaches that God's grace to us doesn't end with our justification. He also makes us his holy children. All his gifts to us give us confidence and power as we work, with him at our side, to fight sin in our lives.

UNIT TWO: YOUR HEART

Lessons 6 through 10 take a closer look at the heart conditions behind our behavior—both sinful behavior and godly living.

LESSON 6: BUT I'M A GOOD PERSON

Big Idea: Two Kinds of Repentance

Often, we may think only "sinners" like the prodigal son need Jesus. But this lesson shows how "older brothers" who are trying to prove themselves to God by being good need to repent as well. Both are given grace by a loving Father.

LESSON 7: DO I *LOVE* GOD? UM . . .

Big Idea: Big Forgiveness and Big Love

When we sin, we have two choices: we can ignore and hide our sin or we can admit it. This lesson teaches that when we learn to admit we're big sinners—who know we have big forgiveness in Jesus—we end up with big love for our Savior.

LESSON 8: YES, I WORSHIP IDOLS

Big Idea: Real-Life Idols

The sins we struggle with show that we have idols in our life. This lesson looks at the things we're tempted to love, trust, or fear more than God—and how Jesus is better than any of those idols.

LESSON 9: LOOK! SHARK!

Big Idea: Confronting Unbelief

It's easy to notice surface sins and try to overcome them, but unless the idols beneath the surface are killed, sin won't be defeated. This lesson examines the dangerous unbelief that lurks below the surface of all our idols and surface sins, and how deeper faith in Jesus is a key part of battling sin.

LESSON 10: THAT'S MY DAD!

Big Idea: Living as God's Child

We claim to be God's children, but how often do we *act* like a son or daughter of the King? This lesson helps us to delight in what it means to have God as our Father, replacing orphan-like behavior with attitudes that fit a child of the King.

UNIT THREE: A CHANGED LIFE

Lessons 11 through 15 examine some of the daily-living results of having a heart that's gripped by the gospel.

LESSON 11: GRRR . . . THAT MAKES ME SO MAD!

Big Idea: Resolving Conflicts

Our sinful desires often lead to conflicts with others. This lesson gives practice in thinking like a child of God, so that from his fatherly promises we draw courage and confidence to resolve those conflicts.

LESSON 12: "I'M SO SORRY—NOT!"

Big Idea: False Repentance

We can feel sorry about sin—and even stop some sin—but that's not necessarily true, godly sorrow and repentance. This lesson shows the selfishness behind false repentance and makes us long for deeper, true repentance.

LESSON 13: I'M SO SORRY—REALLY

Big Idea: Godly Repentance

True repentance sounds hard and often feels impossible. But it's *not* impossible for a child of God, and because of the rich love of our Father, it brings lasting joy. This lesson gives examples of true repentance and encourages us to practice it daily.

LESSON 14: I (GULP) FORGIVE YOU

Big Idea: Forgiving Others

One test that God's grace has made an impact on our hearts is our willingness to forgive. If we've been forgiven *so* much, won't we gladly forgive others? This lesson shows how God's grace enables us to forgive even horribly means things done to us.

LESSON 15: LET'S. KEEP. GOING.

Big Idea: A Lifetime of Faith

Faith isn't just something for the start of the Christian life. It keeps going and growing. This lesson reminds us of many of the important things learned during this course. It helps us consider how to keep going, resting always in Jesus, with the work of faith.

HOW MUCH TIME WILL THE LESSONS TAKE?

If you have 90-minute class sessions, use option 1. If sessions are shorter than 90 minutes, for example, if the curriculum is used in a Sunday school hour, use option 2.

Option 1

Use this option if you have 90-minute class sessions. A full hour and a half provides plenty of time for discussion and prayer, which are important aspects of the course. The sharing and prayer involved in each lesson also mean that smaller groups (or less talkative groups) will tend to finish the lessons more quickly than larger groups. This leader's guide contains time estimates at the beginning of the main parts of each lesson to help keep you on schedule. These assume a fairly large and talkative group.

Option 2

If the class session hovers around one hour, most lessons can be divided and presented in two sessions of 50–55 minutes each. The leader's guide notes the optional break point in each of those lessons and gives instructions on how to wrap up the lesson for the time being and restart it at a later date. Lessons that can be divided are noted with an asterisk in the course overview chart below. If you choose this option, *What's Up?* will encompass 26 class sessions rather than 15.

COURSE OVERVIEW

Option 1: Fifteen 90-minute lessons

Option 2: Twenty-six 50-minute lessons (divided lessons noted with asterisk [*])

Lesson No.	Lesson Title	"Big Idea"	Key Bible passages	Activities	Make It Stick
1*	Oh . . . *Now* I See	Seeing Jesus	Luke 2:10–11; 1 Corinthians 15:1–4	Who, what, why, and how of the gospel; blurry vision	Get to know Jesus
2*	That's My Whole Life Story	The gospel story	Romans 5:12–6:14	Gospel storybook; dying every day	Watch Your Words
3*	My Tongue Is Connected to My—What?	Sin of the heart	Luke 6:45; Genesis 3 (Adam and Eve and the fall); Exodus 32 (Aaron and the golden calf)	Tongue sin motives; Watch Your Words assignment heart attitudes; praying Psalm 139	Watch Your Words (part 2)
4	Hmm . . . What Grades Do I Get?	Justification by faith	Luke 18:9–14 (The Pharisee and the tax collector); 2 Corinthians 5:21	Report card	Teach justification by faith
5*	Presents? For Me?!	Holiness and fighting sin	Ephesians 6:10–18 (The whole armor of God); Psalm 103	Presents from God; using God's armor	Interview an older believer
6*	But I'm a *Good* Person	Two kinds of repentance	Mark 1:15; Luke 15:11–32 (The parable of the lost sons)	Sinners and self-justifiers; lost son character sketches	Spend time with your Father
7*	Do I *Love* God? Um . . .	Big forgiveness and big love	Luke 7:36–47 (Jesus, Simon, and the sinful woman); 1 Corinthians 15:1–4	Two choices when you sin	Admit your sin
8	Yes, I Worship Idols	Real-life idols	Exodus 20:4–5; 1 Kings 18 (Elijah and the priests of Baal); Acts 17:16–34 (Paul in Athens)	What are your idols?	Notice your idol worship
9*	Look! Shark!	Confronting unbelief	Genesis 12:10–19 (Abram in Egypt); Acts 5:1–10 (Ananias and Sapphira); Mark 7:21–23	Shark Figure; praying from Ephesians 3:14–19	The Shark Chart
10*	That's My Dad!	Living as God's child	Galatians 3:26; 2 Samuel 9; 16:1–4; 19:24–30 (David and Mephibosheth)	Benefits of being God's child; living like a son or daughter	Think Like a Son or Daughter
11*	Grrr . . . That Makes Me SO Mad!	Resolving conflicts	Genesis 37–50 (Joseph and his brothers); James 4:1–2	Heart conditions that lead to conflict	Pray for someone
12	I'm So Sorry—NOT!	False repentance	2 Corinthians 7:10; 1 Samuel 15 (Saul disobeys God); Matthew 27:3–10 (Judas has remorse); Micah 6:6–8	Right and wrong ideas about repentance; blurry vision	How I respond to correction
13*	I'm So Sorry—Really!	Godly repentance	Psalm 51 (David's repentance); Luke 15:17–24 (The prodigal son's repentance)	"Not sorry" vs. "Really sorry"; repentance—why do it?	Keep praying for repentance
14*	I (Gulp) Forgive You	Forgiving others	Matthew 18:21–35 (Parable of the unforgiving servant)	Forgiveness stories	Pick a favorite thing you've learned
15	Let's. Keep. Going.	A lifetime of faith	Genesis 22 (Abraham's test of faith); Galatians 3:26–27	The journey of faith; clothed with Christ	

WHAT ARE THE LESSONS LIKE?

Most lessons will have three segments, "Before You Begin," "Today's Lesson," and "Make It Stick."

BEFORE YOU BEGIN includes a review of the previous lesson and a chance to discuss the assignments students worked on since then. Since *What's Up?* is about a student's *whole life*—not just lesson time—the material includes ways to practice faith during the week. Your time with your students will start by discussing how this is going.

TODAY'S LESSON. Lesson time will usually begin with a hook to get students interested, and will include several discussion and workbook pages. *What's Up?* consists of *guided lessons.* As you work through the lessons with your students, there will be activities, discussion questions, and prayer to keep everyone engaged. Your students will often be writing and drawing on their lesson pages: underlining, doodling, matching, writing answers, and drawing pictures. Urge your students to do it all—and model this by marking on your own pages along with them. The pencil work (even if it seems easy) helps students to notice key points in each lesson. The mix of reading, writing, listening, discussing, and doing—using both words and pictures—provides a variety of learning styles to fit all students.

MAKE IT STICK. Lessons end with instructions for practicing faith throughout the week (or however long it is) until you meet again. It's important for students to do these assignments, which is why it's important for YOU always to do them too. Although each student does the work individually, Make It Stick is a *group activity* that'll always be discussed and applied when the group meets. Your experience doing the assignment needs to be part of that in order for you to fully lead that discussion. By joining in that way, you'll also be demonstrating that the practice of faith is a lifetime habit that older believers must engage in every bit as much as young ones. HINT: Make sure each student has a take-home folder for keeping track of Make It Stick assignments. It will help the assignments to get done. We understand, however, that sometimes pages still get lost, folders get forgotten, or students simply choose not to do the work. When this happens, be understanding. Try to involve all students in the Make It Stick discussions even if some failed to complete their pages. You may want to have extra Make It Stick pages on hand for such students to look through or jot thoughts on as they arrive. Your students will appreciate that kind of positive approach to Make It Stick.

This leader's guide includes answers to the exercises in the guided lessons and important themes for you to draw out in discussions. It also alerts you to points in the lesson where you should be prepared to share a personal story. The answers are there to make sure you understand the points each lesson is making. But it's always best to read through the leader's guide and become familiar with those points *ahead of time*, rather than looking up "correct answers" while you and your students are working through the lessons.

WHAT IS THE TEACHER'S ROLE?

Your job is to guide students through the lessons and discussions. You may find it helpful to use a whiteboard to takes notes during discussions, review key points made in the lessons, or write out answers that appear only in your leader's guide. Keep your students engaged. Challenge them to think through the material they're learning. *What's Up?* is not so much about memorizing verses and facts, but about examining the heart. Everything your students learn about the gospel should be connected to their hearts—which connects to how they live each day. Here are some practices that will help:

- Make time for discussions in each session, and share plenty of examples from your own life to illustrate both sin and growth. You need to live "unveiled" before your students. The lessons in *What's Up?* often bring up sin. This is not for the sake of grim brooding, but rather because we believers are confident in our holiness in Christ. This confidence makes us eager to root out sin so we can fight it. Christians *grow*. Secure in Jesus, we are unafraid to drag sin out into the open where it's easier to kill. By modeling this as a leader, you can introduce your students to a lifetime of honesty about their struggles that will help them grow within the Christian community.

- Make prayer central to your sessions with students. Each lesson includes specific times to pray, but you should always be ready to pray more than in those designated spots. If the group or an individual student expresses frustration or concern, that's a good opportunity to take a moment to pray for help. Likewise, if someone tells a success story, that's an opportunity to thank God. Model faith in God and gratitude toward him—not trust in our own abilities—by being a quick-to-pray leader.

- Pray regularly for your students on your own, also. Only the Holy Spirit can open hearts to see God's truth, and only he can bring real growth in your students' lives. Practice what these lessons teach by trusting not in your own ability as a leader but in God's ability to work through you.

- Be aware that there will be struggle. Some students might be indifferent. Others may be so used to **pretending** their way through the Christian life, or **performing** for God, that they will have a difficult time being honest about their faith. When you detect this, keep pointing them back to the gospel. The confidence that in Christ believers are already perfectly, totally loved as children of God can overcome pretending and performing.

HOW WILL MY STUDENTS GROW?

The discipling model used throughout *What's Up?* recognizes that your students must grow from the inside—by *believing the gospel* more deeply—rather than by just *trying harder* to be good outwardly. You may be unfamiliar with this "believe" model. Perhaps you're used to simply helping students discover how they ought to obey God and urging them to do it. If so, it's important that you understand how the "believe" model works.

Jesus said, "This is the work of God, that you believe in him whom he has sent" (John 6:29). Belief in the gospel of Jesus is the soil from which all other obedience grows. This means you will be reminding your students, again and again, to believe first of all. As they believe more deeply in all it means to be joined to Jesus—putting their trust in him rather than in their own performance—they will gain the security, confidence, gratitude, and love for God needed to follow him with abandon.

The following chart, adapted from other Serge materials, summarizes the difference between the "try" model and the "believe" model used in *What's Up?* The "try" model tends to produce self-concerned Christians who are either proud when they perform well or worried when they fail. The "believe" model tends to produce Christ-centered Christians who feel free of the need to make themselves look good—and spend their lives making *him* look good.

	The TRY Model	The BELIEVE Model
The Focus	Behaving on the *outside* Change at the *fruit* level Getting one's act together	Believing on the *inside* Change at the *root* level Obedience from the heart
The Chief Goal	Outward holiness and discipline	Inward love of God and others (1 Timothy 1:5; Galatians 5:6; Matthew 22:40)
The Power	Human effort and moral willpower (Galatians 3:3) "To obey, I *try*"	Faith in Jesus supplies the Spirit (Galatians 3:5) "To obey, I *trust*"
The Dynamic	Buck up! Try harder, get committed "I'm a disappointment"	Believe, submit, trust "I am God's child!"
The Principle	My obedience to God leads to a relationship with him.	My relationship with God leads to obedience to him (John 15:5).
The Motivation	Duty, guilt, pride Determination to be right and look good	Love Passion for the glory of God
Holiness Is . . .	Keeping the rules; doing more for God and doing it better	Loving like Jesus as I believe the gospel more (John 13:34; Romans 13:8f)
"The Flesh" Can Be . . .	Conquered through self-discipline	Conquered through gospel faith, although I'm humbly aware that that my flesh hasn't lost its power
The Leader Must . . .	Model success and competence Appear strong and well-disciplined	Model repentance and trust in Jesus: "I will boast in my weakness so that the power of Christ my rest on me" (2 Corinthians 12:9).
The Student Must . . .	Become a model of how to do more and do it better	Become a big repenter—loving, bold, gracious, and full of faith (1 Timothy 1:15)

Adapted from a chart by Johnny Long based on material from Serge's Grace4Life course.

You are embarking on a teaching experience that aims at the heart and constantly points students to Jesus. You will be showing them the Savior who heals all hurts and fills all longings. With each lesson you'll get to say, like John the Baptist, "Behold, the Lamb of God, who takes away the sin of the world!" (John 1:29). What a breathtaking job you have!

Dear Parent,

Welcome to *What's Up? Discovering the Gospel, Jesus, and Who You Really Are.* This study is designed for middle school (5th–8th grade) students. It encourages them to believe the good news of Jesus and live it out.

We are grateful for the opportunity to partner with you in the discipleship of your child. *What's Up?* is designed for a group study and each lesson builds on the others. If your child misses a session, he or she can complete the missed lesson at home, but may need some parental guidance and support. Likewise, if your child wants to do *What's Up?* individually, you (or some other adult mentor) should become the "group" and review the lessons alongside your child.

In either case, if you think you will be guiding your child through some lessons, you should obtain a leader's edition of *What's Up?* The *Teacher Guide* contains instructions and explanations that help you through the lessons and activities. The *Teacher Guide* also gives detailed explanations of what your child will be learning and how the group sessions are conducted. Even if you don't plan on leading your child through any of the lessons, having your own copy may help you follow up on the teaching at home without having to look through your child's student workbook, which may contain private reflections.

You may find that *What's Up?* challenges your child to live as a believer in ways he or she has seldom considered before. There will be Make It Stick assignments for home that require prayer, Bible reading, discussions with others about Jesus, and more—often on a daily basis. Your support and encouragement will be important if your child is to get the maximum benefit from these assignments. It may help to ask your child about these assignments during the week or to remind him or her to bring the *Student Guide* to each class.

Our prayer is that throughout the *What's Up?* study you and your child's love for Jesus will grow. May God bless and encourage you as you study together.

Blessings in Christ,
Debbie and Jack

INTRODUCTION

IS *WHAT'S UP?* FOR ME?

Yes, it's for you if you want to learn more about Jesus or grow in your life with him. Maybe you only know a little bit about the Bible, and want to learn what believing in Jesus means. *What's Up?* will teach you what it's all about—and show you how to get started, if that's what you decide. Or maybe you've heard and read the Bible so much that you know every story by heart, but now you want to live it out. *What's Up?* will help you look to Jesus and delight in all he's done for you—and believe!

BUT WHAT IF I ALREADY BELIEVE?

That's great! But faith must always grow. You know that you often fail to be kind in how you treat your friends, classmates, parents, and teachers. *What's Up?* will teach you not to hide or ignore that sin, but to admit it and trust Jesus. You'll learn to enjoy how he always forgives you. You'll believe more deeply that he died for you and made you God's holy, ever-welcomed child. You'll learn to live the way someone who believes those things ought to live. That's growing in faith!

WILL IT MAKE ANY DIFFERENCE IN MY LIFE?

Oh, if you come to know you're God's child, it makes *all* the difference. It gives you love for your Father so you want to live for him. You'll see how much he cares for you and for *everything* you do, so that you become excited about life with Jesus. It also gives you confidence that God is on your side—even when you fail! You can stop being scared of God when you've sinned and instead go to him for help. You'll not only learn to resist sin that way; you'll learn to constantly trust and live close to Jesus. *What's Up?* won't just change how you think as a child of God. It should also change how you *act* as a child of God.

WHAT WILL I BE DOING?

You'll work through your lesson pages with a Bible and a pen or pencil. *What's Up?* will guide you as you rely on God to help your faith grow. You'll spend much time using the tools *he* gives you to help you learn. Here's what you'll use:

The Bible. God speaks to you through the Bible. These lessons will use the Bible to teach you and will get you reading your Bible.

Prayer. Prayer is how you talk to God and ask him for help. Since you need God's help to grow, the lessons and assignments in *What's Up?* will include lots of prayer.

The good news of Jesus. Jesus and all he does for us are the main message of the Bible, so *What's Up?* will keep mentioning this good news again and again. You need to keep remembering and believing it.

Other believers. God makes believers in Jesus part of his family so they can help each other grow more faithful. These lessons will get you sharing with a group, talking about your faith with others, and learning from an experienced leader.

WHAT IF I DON'T HAVE A GROUP?

The lessons are designed for group study. Sharing with others in a group will be the best way for you to learn the most from *What's Up?* If you don't have a group, you can still do the study by yourself, but even then you need to find an adult leader to be your mentor and guide you through the lessons. That person will be who you share with—and will also share *their* stories with *you*. This kind of sharing is an important part of *What's Up?*

WHAT WILL THE LESSONS BE LIKE?

Most lessons will have three segments:

BEFORE YOU BEGIN. Since *What's Up?* is about your whole life—not just lesson time—you'll start by talking about your life! You share what you've learned and how you've been practicing faith since the last time your group met.

TODAY'S LESSON. Lesson time will include several discussion and workbook pages. *What's Up?* keeps you doing stuff all through the lesson. You'll be writing and drawing on your lesson pages: underlining, doodling, matching, writing answers, and drawing pictures—that kind of thing. You'll also read from the Bible, discuss the lesson with your group, and pray.

Important note: You might think discussing your faith and praying is TOO HARD. Try it anyway. It gets easier with practice, and it's an important part of Christian growth.

MORE important note: You might think underlining, circling, and writing answers on your lesson pages is TOO EASY. Do it anyway. Of course it's easy, but it's the best way for you to notice what you're learning—like taking notes. (Besides, you get to write, draw, and doodle on your lessons, which is sweet!)

MAKE IT STICK. Here you'll get directions for practicing what you learned during the week. It's important to always do the Make It Stick assignment during the week. It's what makes *What's Up?* about your whole life. Plus, you'll be reporting how it went the next time you meet with your group. Even though Make It Stick is something you'll do at home on your own, it's still a group activity that'll end up helping the whole group when you discuss it together later.

ANOTHER important note: Make It Stick is *practice*. *What's Up?* is a discipleship course. It trains you in how to live. That's why daily practice, and sharing with your group how it went, is so important.

WHAT ELSE SHOULD I EXPECT?

Expect God to work in you. He loves you. Jesus died on the cross to save all who believe in him. "He gave his life to free us from every kind of sin, to cleanse us, and to make us his very own people, totally committed to doing good deeds" (Titus 2:14 NLT). Start praying now that God will use *What's Up?* to help make everything that verse says true of *you*. God is determined that his people will grow. Look forward to it.

OH... NOW I SEE

Big Idea: Seeing Jesus

NOTES TO THE LEADER

LESSON GOAL

Students will see that Christianity is about good news—the gospel—and that this news is first of all about what Jesus does for us, not what we must do for God.

SUMMARY

This lesson begins by giving students a chance to say what they think God and Christianity are all about. This exercise not only introduces the topic, but also gives you the opportunity to begin learning how each student approaches God and faith. The lesson uses the theme of "clear vision" and "blurry" vision to talk about right and wrong ways to think about the gospel.

In PART 1, Clear Vision, students examine Bible passages that tell about the gospel.

- ★ *The gospel is about Jesus (Whom is it about?)*

- ★ *The gospel is about God's plan for salvation. (What does Jesus do for us?)*

- ★ *The gospel says our salvation is a gift from God; we cannot earn it. (How are we saved from sin?)*

- ★ *The gospel says we are saved because God loves us. (Why does God save us?)*

- ★ *Our response to the gospel should be to believe in Jesus. (How do I respond?)*

PART 2, Blurry Vision, examines our wrong ideas about Jesus and salvation. You will see some familiar, blurry ways of thinking, and diagnose what's missing from view. You will have a chance to share how you sometimes fail to see the gospel clearly. You will pray for better vision.

SUPPLEMENTAL FIGURE

You'll be using the Blurry Gospel Vision Figure in part 2 of this lesson.

YOUR PREPARATION

STUDY. Read through the lesson and teaching notes and make sure you understand it all before class begins. Also be prepared to explain the gospel, and what's entailed in believing it, in your own words. Keep this in mind: Lessons like this one that explain the gospel are ideal for both believers and unbelievers. Some of your students may not yet have faith in Jesus. This lesson will show them what it means to believe. Other students may already be believers. This lesson will encourage them to sharpen and deepen their belief. It is not necessary for you to identify nonbelievers and target them for special treatment. Both kinds of students must be encouraged to believe the gospel—whether for the first time or more deeply. Be prepared to talk to all your students about what this means. It's about faith (trusting Jesus, not your own goodness) and repentance (living for Jesus, not yourself), and it's for everyone, all the time.

BE READY TO SHARE. One of the features of this course is honest, open discussion about our own sins, faults, and questions. Encourage your students to share openly by participating yourself. In this lesson, you'll have an opportunity near the end to tell what sort of "blurry vision" of the gospel you sometimes fall into. Be sure you've looked at the examples ahead of time and are ready to share which one is most like you. Have a specific example of how it applies in your Christian life and how you need to constantly work to improve your "vision" in that area.

PRAY. The first class session usually sets a tone for those to come. Ask your Father to make your students eager to hear the gospel and willing to share openly. Pray that the Spirit would penetrate the hearts of your students—and your own heart—with his good news.

BEFORE YOU BEGIN

(20 minutes)

Together, read the student introduction to What's Up? It's important that your students understand the goals of this course and why the lessons will ask them to share, pray, write down answers, and do the Make It Stick assignments.

In these lessons, you're going to learn about God from the Bible. Maybe you're wondering: what are the basic facts about who God is?

- Use the God Fact Sheet to get you started. To keep it fun, do this:
- Check off things you already knew about God. (✔)
- Put a star next to things you might have heard before, but weren't sure about.
- Write "wow!" next to anything that's brand new to you. *WOW!*

THE GOD FACT SHEET

ONE God. There is only one God. He's a spiritual being, and he created *everything* that exists.

- ☐ God is eternal. He was never created. He has always existed and always will exist.
- ☐ God is all-powerful. He knows and controls everything.
- ☐ God is holy. He's perfect and pure of any evil, which he calls "sin." He never sins and can't stand sin.

THREE persons. Even though God is only one, he exists as three persons—the Father, the Son, and the Holy Spirit. Each person is *all the way* God (eternal Creator, all-powerful, perfect, and holy). These three persons . . .

- ☐ Communicate with each other.
- ☐ Make agreements with each other (they never disagree, because God is one).
- ☐ Love each other (perfectly, of course).

Our Savior. The three persons work together in everything, including acting together to save us from our sin. They each have a special role in saving us.

- ☐ The Father lovingly ordered our salvation and sent the Son to be our Savior.
- ☐ The Son accomplished our salvation by taking the punishment that we deserved for our sin.
- ☐ The Holy Spirit changes us so we can be saved by believing that the Son died for us. He also teaches us to resist sin and live for God.

Jesus. To be our Savior, about 2,000 years ago the Son became a human being—without stopping to still be *all the way* God too. He was born and took the name Jesus. Jesus is both God and also *all the way* a man! As a man, there are things about him that ordinarily wouldn't be true of God.

- ☐ Jesus got tired, hungry, and thirsty. He also has every human emotion (but only in non-sinning ways, since he's still holy God).
- ☐ Jesus was tempted to sin, like we are (but he never did sin).
- ☐ Jesus suffered and died before being raised to life again.

Now tell the rest of the group what you learned from the God Fact Sheet. What was really interesting to you? Was anything confusing?

Let's do one thing more. Before starting these lessons you probably already have an idea about what Christianity is. So think of a word or short phrase that describes being a Christian and then tell what you wrote.

Christianity is _____

_____

_____.

Let students share openly. Don't judge answers as better or worse at this point.

TODAY'S LESSON

In this lesson, you'll learn a word *Jesus* chose to describe what he's all about. First, you'll learn what this word is. You'll also get a "clear vision" view of why it makes being a Christian different from what many people think.

Then, in the second part of this lesson, you'll compare that word to other ideas and feelings you might have about God—"blurry vision" ones.

PART 1: EXACTLY THE RIGHT WORD

(25 minutes)

When Jesus lived on earth, he picked a word to explain what his work was all about. He chose the word "gospel." It means "good news." In those days, no one had ever used that word for religion! It was used for good news brought by a king's messenger—like news of a battle won. It was news everyone would be glad to hear and let change their life. Our Bibles sometimes use the word "gospel" and sometimes say "good news," but they're the same thing.

 Point to remember: "Gospel" means GOOD NEWS!

Let's see what the Bible says about this good news.

You may have heard about the angel who told shepherds about baby Jesus. That angel was being a messenger, bringing good news—the gospel!

And the angel said to them, "Fear not, for behold, I bring you good news of great joy that will be for all the people. For unto you is born this day in the city of David a Savior, who is Christ the Lord." (Luke 2:10–11)

Find "good news" in those verses and **it.**

Then find the word "Savior" and put a star next to it.

Finally, <u>underline</u> the part of the angel's message that tells WHOM the gospel is all about.

The missionary Paul wrote about the gospel in the Bible. Read what he said.

> Now I would remind you, brothers, of the gospel I preached to you, which you received, in which you stand, and by which you are being saved, if you hold fast to the word I preached to you—unless you believed in vain.
>
> For I delivered to you as of first importance what I also received: that Christ died for our sins in accordance with the Scriptures, that he was buried, that he was raised on the third day in accordance with the Scriptures. (1 Corinthians 15:1–4)

Again, circle the word "gospel."

Find the part where Paul says the gospel is about being saved and put a star by it. ★

And <u>underline</u> the sentence that tells WHOM the gospel is about and what he did for us.

The gospel is news about the Christ (that's a title for JESUS). It's about how he SAVES US.

You're ready to start filling in your "clear vision" view of the gospel. Start by writing WHOM the gospel is about on the blank eyeglass lens that follows.

Students should see that the gospel is about Jesus, or the Christ. If any are confused by the term "Christ," you can explain that it means "anointed" and is a title for Jesus, like "president" might be a title for a nation's leader.

Now fill in WHAT Jesus does for us in the gospel. (Hint: It's what you put the stars by in our verses.)

Students should see that the gospel is about salvation. Jesus saves us.

‐ ‐ ‐ ‐ ‐ ‐ ‐ ‐ ‐ ‐ ‐ ‐ ‐ ‐ ‐ ‐ ‐ ‐ ‐

★ THE ★ GOSPEL

WHAT does Jesus do for us?

TALK ABOUT IT

Most of the time, do you feel like you need Jesus to save you from anything? Why or why not? When do you most feel like you need a Savior?

Some students may deeply feel the weight of their sin and their need for Jesus, while other students may have never even considered it. Encourage them not just to give an answer they think is "right," but to consider whether or not they daily realize their need. At this point, you don't need to "beat them over the head" with their sin if they have little awareness. Simply accept that this is often the case and tell them that noticing their sin will be a big part of these lessons—because we want to be honest about ourselves and come to appreciate how important Jesus is.

<u>Remember that "sin" means we do evil things that are against God. We deserve to be punished.</u>

Find Romans 3:23–24 in your Bible. Read it to learn more about what it means to be saved. Then write an answer to the question below.

HOW are we saved from sin? Is it because we earn *it* by being good and not sinning, or is it a *gift* God gives us through Jesus? Fill in the eyeglasses with your answer.

 Salvation is "by grace" or "as a gift" or "not earned."
_ _ _ _ _ _ _ _ _ _ _ _ _ _ _ _ _

HOW are we saved from sin?

Now read one more Bible verse that tells about being saved. Look up John 3:16 and answer the two questions below.

WHY did God decide to give his Son, Jesus, to save us? HOW do you respond in order to have eternal life?

Believing in Jesus includes:

- **Trusting Jesus** instead of trying to be good enough to save yourself.
- **Living for Jesus** and obeying him instead of living for yourself.

Now use your answers to fill in the last parts of your gospel vision. Start by writing WHY God saves us, as a gift, through Jesus.

 God's reason for saving us is his love.
_ _ _ _ _ _ _ _ _ _ _ _ _ _ _

WHY does God save us?

★ 17

Finally, write what you do to respond to this good news.

Now let's combine what you've learned about the gospel with what you know about God:

GOD IS HOLY. He hates sin. Since you're a sinner who does wrong every day, you need to be saved from sin to be accepted by a holy God.

GOD IS FAIR. He punishes sin. Sinners must die. So *you* must be punished unless <u>someone else</u> who's perfectly good takes your place as a substitute.

GOD IS LOVING. He gave his Son, Jesus, to be that <u>someone else</u>. Jesus was punished instead of you—in your place!—if you believe in him. This means you can be accepted by God even though you sin.

TALK ABOUT IT

Discuss the three points listed above. Which do you most often hear people talk about? Which are new to you or are ideas you don't think about much? Explain why *all three* are important.

Help students to see how all three ideas are necessary to the gospel. It may be helpful to review the points by writing out a simple chart like the one below. Your student may be able to fill in the right half of the chart that tells what the gospel means.

GOD IS . . .   THE GOSPEL MEANS . . .

GOD IS . . .	THE GOSPEL MEANS . . .
Holy and without sin	I am a sinner. I need to be saved.
Fair. Sin must be punished.	I need someone to take the punishment I deserve for my sin.
Love	God sent his son, Jesus, to take the punishment I deserve.

TEST YOURSELF

Circle the believer in each pair of students who has "clear vision" of the gospel, and tell why.

Use this "test" as one more opportunity to discuss key points of the gospel with your students. For each set of statements, ask the group which student sees the gospel clearly and have a student or two explain why.

GOOD NEWS

"Christianity is mostly about what I have to do for God."

"Christianity is first of all about good news of what God does for me!"

The gospel is first of all news about what God does for us. This doesn't mean that our obedience to God is unimportant, but our obedience flows from the work of Jesus on our behalf. His work is primary.

WHY?_____

_____

_____

SIN

"I'm a far worse sinner than I thought. I offend the holy God so often! No matter how hard I try, I can't make myself good enough for him."

"As long as I try hard to be good, God shouldn't think of me as too bad a sinner."

The key here is to understand that God is holy—perfectly good—so that our sins are rightfully a great offense to him.

WHY?_____

★ ACCEPTED ★

"God accepts me whenever I'm good like I should be, and he gets grumpy with me when I'm not."

"God accepts me because Jesus is good, and I belong to Jesus. He took the punishment I deserve."

Although our behavior varies in its acceptability based on how good we are, God's eternal acceptance of us is based on the goodness of Jesus—and that never changes. The good works we do as believers are only truly good and only please God at all because we are joined to Jesus. And even then, we're not counted righteous (justified) because of those good works but rather because we belong to Jesus and he is good.

WHY?_____

"Jesus loves me. He died for me! Now I obey him because he means everything to me."

JESUS

"I need to obey Jesus better if I want him to like me."

A believer is eager to please God, but that good behavior flows from Christ's love to him. It's not a scheme to earn or merit God's favor.

WHY?_____

BELIEVE IT!

"Believing in Jesus means that now I both trust him and live for him eagerly, every day. It changes everything!"

"Believing in Jesus means I can go on with my life and hardly have to think about my sin anymore. I'm glad it's so easy and doesn't require much change!"

Your students may think that the freeness of the gospel means they can go on with their lives and just forget about their sin, but such thinking is wrong. Belief in Jesus is such a change of life that, by the work of the Holy Spirit in us, it brings transformation into people who fight against sin and live for God. It changes everything.

WHY?_____

★ 21

OPTIONAL STOPPING POINT

If you're stopping the lesson here for today, send your students home with *something to think about* and *prayer*.

SOMETHING TO THINK ABOUT

Tell students: This week see if you can remember the five questions about the gospel and their answers. Here they are again:

- ★ *Who is the gospel about? (The gospel is about Jesus.)*
- ★ *What does Jesus do for us? (He saves us.)*
- ★ *How does Jesus save us? (Our salvation is a gift from God; we cannot earn it.)*
- ★ *Why does God save us? (Because he God loves us.)*
- ★ *How do I respond? (By believing in Jesus.)*

Quickly write down the answers if you have to. Learn them and be ready to answer those questions at the start of your next class.

PRAYER

Pray together that the Holy Spirit would help bring you and your students a deeper understanding of the gospel.

When you restart this lesson later, begin with *review*.

REVIEW

Ask students the five questions they responded to last time. Review the answers. Also ask: Did you learn something new about the gospel that you didn't know before? Do these answers change the way you view Christianity?

PART 2: BLURRY VISION

(40 minutes. Leave plenty of time for discussion and prayer at the end of this part of the lesson.)

Seeing the gospel clearly is like an eye exam. Even if you already know about the gospel, sometimes your vision can get "blurry." So now, *you be the eye doctor*. For each student, find what that student <u>can't see</u> about the gospel.

Maybe it's . . .

☑ What a big sinner they are

☑ How God accepts them because of Jesus, not how good or bad they are

☑ How Jesus loves them and died for their sin

☑ How believing the gospel means a new, changed life

Then, once that student has a "prescription" to see the gospel more clearly, describe how you think their life will change.

THE SMUG STUDENT

"Sometimes I sin, but I'm better than most people. I study the Bible and I obey at school; and I'm sure God has noticed. There are bad people who need Jesus much worse than I do. God is glad that I'm one of the good guys!"

BLURRY VISION

This student <u>can't see</u> (check what applies):

☐ They're a big sinner just like everyone else.

☐ God accepts them because of Jesus, not how good they are.

☐ Jesus loves them and died for their sin.

☐ Believing in Jesus means a new, changed life.

PRESCRIPTION

THE GOSPEL SAYS: You're a big sinner too. God only accepts you because of Jesus, not how good you think you are.

LIFE WITH GOSPEL VISION

When you see the gospel, you'll stop bragging and being proud. You'll quit trying to prove how good you are. Instead, you'll . . .

_____

_____

_____.

THE NERVOUS STUDENT

"I get worried when I think about Jesus. I know he wants me to shape up and live better, and I've tried. But I'm pretty sure that I'm not good enough and God stays pretty unhappy with me. When I sin, I try to make it up to God by doing something good. I'll keep trying and hope God will be okay with that."

BLURRY VISION

This student <u>can't see</u> (check what applies):

❑ They're a big sinner just like everyone else.

❑ God accepts them because of Jesus, not how good they are.

❑ Jesus loves them and died for their sin.

❑ Believing in Jesus means a new, changed life.

PRESCRIPTION

THE GOSPEL SAYS: You don't have to earn your forgiveness. God accepts you because of Jesus. It's free!

LIFE WITH GOSPEL VISION

When you see the gospel, you'll stop worrying and being secretly scared of God. You'll quit doing good things only because you feel pressure. Instead, you'll . . .

_____

_____.

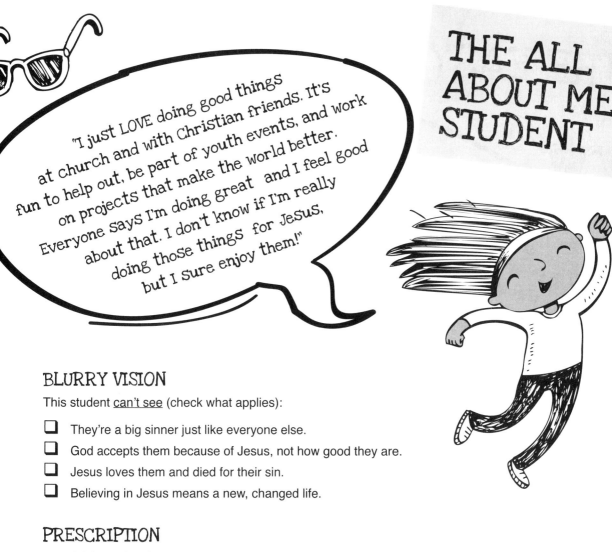

"I just LOVE doing good things at church and with Christian friends. It's fun to help out, be part of youth events, and work on projects that make the world better. Everyone says I'm doing great and I feel good about that. I don't know if I'm really doing those things for Jesus, but I sure enjoy them!"

BLURRY VISION

This student <u>can't see</u> (check what applies):

☐ They're a big sinner just like everyone else.

☐ God accepts them because of Jesus, not how good they are.

☐ Jesus loves them and died for their sin.

☐ Believing in Jesus means a new, changed life.

PRESCRIPTION

THE GOSPEL SAYS: Jesus died for you. He loves you *that* much! *He's* the best reason to serve God.

LIFE WITH GOSPEL VISION

When you see the gospel, you'll stop doing godly-looking things just because they're fun, or because people are watching. Instead, you'll . . .

_____

_____

_____ .

The student can't see that Jesus loves them and died for their sin. Make sure your students recognize that this student is really doing all those good things for himself, not because Jesus is his Savior. Those with gospel vision will do godly things because they're committed to Jesus even when it isn't fun. They will thankfully live for him even when no one else is watching. They will become selfless.

NOTE: Your students may argue that it's good to enjoy doing good things. They're right about that, of course. Try to help them see, though, that the ALL ABOUT ME student is only doing things he'd enjoy anyway even without Jesus. The gospel must bring repentance: those who believe the gospel change how they would otherwise live and do so out of their gladness in Jesus. Even though the ALL ABOUT ME student is outwardly more godly than the EASY LIFE student (discussed next), neither is repenting because of Jesus.

THE EASY LIFE STUDENT

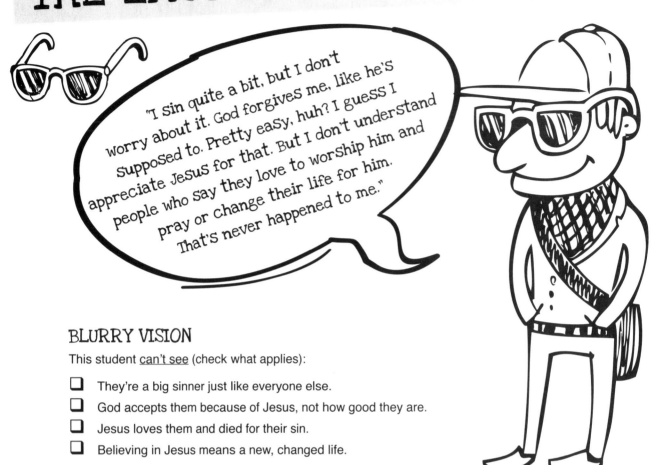

"I sin quite a bit, but I don't worry about it. God forgives me, like he's supposed to. Pretty easy, huh? I guess I appreciate Jesus for that. But I don't understand people who say they love to worship him and pray or change their life for him. That's never happened to me."

BLURRY VISION

This student <u>can't see</u> (check what applies):

- ☐ They're a big sinner just like everyone else.
- ☐ God accepts them because of Jesus, not how good they are.
- ☐ Jesus loves them and died for their sin.
- ☐ Believing in Jesus means a new, changed life.

PRESCRIPTION

THE GOSPEL SAYS: Believing in Jesus means your life isn't about yourself anymore. You don't trust yourself. You don't live for yourself, either. You change so that you trust and live for Jesus, instead.

LIFE WITH GOSPEL VISION

When you see the gospel, you'll no longer have a self-centered life that finds Jesus boring. Instead, you'll . . .

_____

_____

_____ .

The student can't see that believing in Jesus means a new, changed life. But those with gospel vision will repent of their sin, will be thankful to Jesus and eager to serve him, will pray and grow as believers, and will become joyful over Jesus and find worshiping him to be a thrill.

BLURRY GOSPEL VISION

which blurry vision student are you most like?

THE SMUG ONE

"Yes, sometimes I sin, but I'm better than most people. I do Bible studies and I obey at school, and I'm sure God has noticed. There are bad people who need Jesus much worse than I do."

YOU CAN'T SEE
You're a big sinner—much worse than you think!—especially in how you look down on others.

GOSPEL PRESCRIPTION
You're a big sinner just like everyone else. God only accepts anyone because of Jesus, never because of how good they are.

Your life with GOSPEL vision:
You stop being proud and start to treasure Jesus. It's he who gives you a good reputation with God, so you no longer feel a need to prove how good you are. You stop bragging and learn to care about others.

THE NERVOUS ONE

"I don't always admit it, but I'm secretly worried that I'm not good enough for God. When I sin, I try to make it up to God by doing something good. I'll keep trying and hope God's okay with that."

YOU CAN'T SEE
God loves and accepts you even though you still sin.

GOSPEL PRESCRIPTION
God loves you even though you still sin. Jesus took your place. You don't have to earn your forgiveness. It's free!

Your life with GOSPEL vision:
You stop feeling worried and learn to rest in God's love. This lets you love God back instead of being scared of him. You start to do good things eagerly— out of thankfulness, not due to pressure.

THE ALL ABOUT ME ONE

"I just LOVE doing good things at church and with my friends. It's fun to be part of youth events and to do things that make the world better. Everyone says I'm doing great—so I guess I am!"

YOU CAN'T SEE
Jesus has died for you. You're just doing good things because you enjoy them and they make you feel good about yourself—not really for Jesus.

GOSPEL PRESCRIPTION
Jesus died for you. He loves you *that* much!

Your life with GOSPEL vision:
The reason why you enjoy doing good things changes. You start to do them because you're glad to be repenting— Changing your life out of love for Jesus. You're eager to serve him even when it isn't fun and you live for him even when no one is watching.

THE EASY LIFE ONE

"I don't worry about my sin. God forgives me, like he's supposed to. Pretty easy, huh I appreciate Jesus for that, but I don't understand people who say they love to worship him and pray. That's never happened to me."

YOU CAN'T SEE
The gospel must change everything about how you live. It's bigger than cheap forgiveness.

GOSPEL PRESCRIPTION
Your sin was not easy to fix and the change Jesus brings is huge. He *died* to give you *new life*. Now the Spirit makes you able to live for him—and to love it!

Your life with GOSPEL vision:
You're thankful to Jesus and eager to fully enjoy your new life with him. You pray often, trusting the Spirit to help you grow. Since Jesus is all-important to you, worshiping him is not boring.

Looking at the Blurry Gospel Vision figure, think about each student with "blurry vision." Which one is most like *you*? Once you pick which one you're most like, circle it, and share your choice with the group. Explain how your way of thinking about God is sometimes like that blurry vision.

Encourage students to carefully read through the descriptions again and pick the one that's most like them. They may have a hard time picking just one, but encourage them to think about their hearts and zero in on the choice that best describes them. Being forced to choose one main tendency will help them to consider the question carefully, and their choice will guide their prayer that's coming up.

SHARING OPPORTUNITY: This discussion is the first of many in the course that requires students to admit their shortcomings. It's essential that you, as the leader, show that this is okay by sharing which student you're most like and by participating in prayer the prayer that follows, asking God that you too would better see the gospel.

PRAY ABOUT IT

Remember how the Holy Spirit helps us believe the gospel? Everyone needs clearer gospel vision—even people who've believed the gospel for many years! So now, ask God to help you. Pray with a friend or by yourself. Here's how to do it:

Look back at the type of blurry vision you circled. Then look at the final box labeled "your life with gospel vision."

Pray for the things written in that box to happen to you. Pray that the Holy Spirit will change you so that those things become true of you as you learn and believe the gospel through these lessons.

You can either say your prayer aloud or write it out in a few sentences below.

_____

_____

_____

_____

_____.

Take this prayer time seriously. It sets the tone for the rest of the course, and it is one way we practice believing the gospel. Applying the lessons in this course is not first about our efforts, but rather about relying on God's work in us—so we will pray often!

NOTE: As you learned what believing the gospel means, you may have thought to yourself: "Hmm, I'm not sure I've ever actually believed the gospel." If that's the case with you, consider becoming a believer. You can start believing (by trusting Jesus to save you and deciding to live for him) at any time—the sooner the better! But as you've learned, it's an important decision that you need to consider carefully and take seriously. The rest of our lessons will help you learn more about what it means to be a believer.

The rest of the lessons will also speak to you as if you already *are* a believer. Those who believe in Jesus are forgiven, have become God's children, have eternal life—and more! These lessons will help believers to believe these things more deeply, so they can grow. If you actually aren't a believer yet, you too can learn about Jesus and all he does for us. Our hope is that you will come to believe for the first time—and then keep believing more deeply all your life.

MAKE IT STICK:

GET TO KNOW JESUS

(Take 5 minutes at the end of the session to explain the coming week's "Make It Stick" exercise.)

INSTRUCTIONS:

Fill out this Make It Stick page during the week.

Don't forget to bring your *Student Guide* back next time you meet.

If you have time, go ahead and get started now.

Jesus isn't just a way to be forgiven and accepted by God. He's also a person—the *best* person you could ever know! So before the next time you meet, practice getting to know Jesus better by reading about him in the Bible and noticing what kind of man he is.

Start by reading **Luke 7:11–17**. It's a short account of a time when Jesus visited a town called Nain. Read what happened there.

Then, on the lines below, write words or short phrases that tell what kind of person Jesus is—based on just this one, short story. Look closely at the details in the story and fill out as many lines as you can. It might help to consider these questions:

What abilities does he have?
How does he treat people?
What does he feel?
What are his attitudes?
What surprises you about his behavior?
How is he different from you?

(You don't have to answer each question. Just use them to help you think of some words that describe Jesus.)

_____

_____

_____

_____

_____

_____

Be ready to share what you noticed about Jesus the next time you meet.

LESSON 2

THAT'S MY WHOLE LIFE STORY

Big Idea: The Gospel Story

LESSON GOAL

Students will learn the gospel story of creation, the fall, and redemption in Jesus. They'll come to appreciate how those who are joined to Jesus have been part of that story from the beginning—and will be forever.

SUMMARY

The first lesson introduced the basic idea of the gospel in terms of how we are saved. This one puts that in context by telling the story of salvation in Jesus from beginning to end. The lesson is presented as chapters in a picture storybook. In each chapter, your students will be encouraged to draw themselves into the picture as they learn how, joined to Jesus, the story is about them as well.

CHAPTER 1: God's Perfect World. God created a sinless world and made people in his image. Already then, God had chosen believers to be created in the likeness of Jesus to glorify God and enjoy him forever.

CHAPTER 2: Rebellion. Mankind disobeyed God and became his enemies, deserving punishment. In Adam, we all have sinned.

CHAPTER 3: The Gospel. The Son of God, Jesus, obeyed perfectly but took the punishment we deserve; then rose from the dead and rules from heaven. Those who believe in him also have their old selves crucified, have new life, and are seated with him in heaven.

CHAPTER 4: Your Life Today. Believers are now children of God who serve Jesus. Joined forever to him, they daily die to self as they await his return.

As you work through each chapter, help your students see the richness of being joined to Jesus. An appreciation of him as a stunning person they're joined to forever will help him

become to them much more than just a way to be saved. He'll become a friend they're eager to live with, and a Lord they're eager to live for.

YOUR PREPARATION

STUDY. Read the entire lesson and the teaching notes and get a good understanding of what it teaches. Since union with Christ is a theological topic many teachers haven't studied in depth, you should also read some of the key Bible passages that speak of it. Doing so will help you understand the concept and speak of it to your students with excitement. So read through:

★ *Ephesians 2:1–10. (Themes: Our dead state, our life in Christ, being seated with Christ, being created in Christ)*

★ *Romans 5:12—6:13. (Themes: Our old life crucified with Christ, our new life alive in Christ)*

★ *1 Corinthians 15:20–22. (Themes: Death through Adam, resurrection through Christ)*

As you read, be sure to notice how being joined to Jesus makes a difference in how we live.

BE READY TO SHARE. Be sure you've done the assignment from the end of the first lesson and are ready to share what you've learned, just as you expect your students to share. In addition, be prepared to give an example of a temptation you commonly face and what you do instead of giving in to that temptation—because you're joined to Jesus. That opportunity will come near the end of the lesson, following "Chapter 4" of the storybook.

PRAY. As you prepare, pray that the gospel story, which you may feel you already know well, would become fresh and new to you as you study it and get ready to teach it. Pray that God would help you to see new things that get you excited about Jesus. Pray the same for your students—especially those who may think the story is old news to them.

BEFORE YOU BEGIN

(About 15 minutes)

Remember what you learned last time. Jesus brought the GOSPEL. It means GOOD NEWS.

Look back to the start of lesson one. What was the word you wrote down to describe Christianity near the beginning of that lesson? How does the gospel compare to the word you picked?

The purpose of this question is to review that last lesson, not to see who had the best answer. Help students compare what they've learned with the words they were thinking of at the start of that first lesson. Many of the words they picked may be similar to the gospel. Others may be part of Christianity, but not central to it the way "gospel" is. Rather than drawing attention to their best or worst choices, remind the students that our experiences with Christianity give all of us "blurry vision" sometimes when it comes to the gospel. That's why we keep studying it.

Jesus is both our Savior (one who saves us from sin) and an amazing person. Share what you learned about him from reading Luke 7:11–17. What are some of the words you used to describe him?

What do you think is the *most amazing* thing about the kind of person Jesus is—the thing that most makes you want to know him better and live your life for him?

Allow students to share what they think. Be sure that you, as the leader, did the exercise too and are prepared to share something you found amazing about Jesus.

TODAY'S LESSON

(70 minutes—approximately 30 minutes for "Chapters" 1 and 2 and 40 minutes for "Chapters" 3 and 4.)

Don't you just love a great story, one you can't put down!

Imagine a character in such a story is in a life or death situation. They can't get out on their own. They need a hero to rescue them.

As you read you suddenly realize that character is you! You can't get out on your own. You need a hero. The story you're reading is the true story of how Jesus called you to believe in him, to rescue you.

Jesus is the main character in the big, true story told in the whole Bible. Plus, he's *your* Savior if you believe in him. In this lesson, you'll learn his story—the story of how we've sinned and are saved by Jesus. It's your story too.

Let's take the story chapter by chapter, like in one of those picture storybooks you had when you were a kid. (If you're working in a group, it'll probably work best to read each section of the story and fill in the blanks together.)

Encourage students to be creative; they can draw a detailed or a stick figure of themselves into the picture.

CHAPTER 1: GOD'S PERFECT WORLD

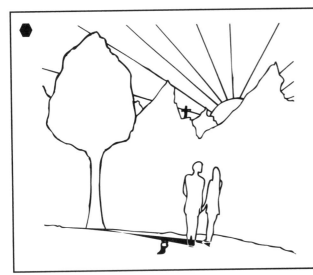

Everything began with God—Father, Son and Holy Spirit—each person loving and honoring the others. His creation was like him, perfect and without the slightest sin. God filled the world with his beauty and his glory. From the first twinkling star to the massive whales that navigate the oceans, all of God's creation was good. People were most special of all.

> God created man in his own image, in the image of God he created him; male and female he created them. (Genesis 1:27)
>
> "Everyone who is called by my name, whom I created for my glory, whom I formed and made." (Isaiah 43:7)

What do the Bible passages say people were like when God created them?

They were in God's image/likeness

created to be good like him. They were

called by his name.

What does Isaiah 43:7 say people were created for?

For God's glory.

It is easy to read the creation story and think, "This has nothing to do with me. It happened long before I was even born." But read what the Bible says about how *you* were part of that story too, way back in the beginning.

> [God] chose us in him before the foundation of the world, that we should be holy and blameless before him. (Ephesians 1:4)
>
> Put on the new self, created after the likeness of God in true righteousness and holiness. (Ephesians 4:24)

God chose you to be in this story and planned to rescue you. You too are created to glorify him and enjoy him forever—to be with him and be like him, holy and blameless.

So to remind yourself that God created you to be LIKE HIM and WITH HIM, <u>add yourself to the story by drawing a picture of yourself in the creation picture above</u>. Then fill in the blanks below.

"God created me in his own

image/likeness

to be _holy/blameless_ .

My purpose is to

glorify and enjoy -or- be like him."

TALK ABOUT IT

Share how it feels to know *you* were created to be like God, holy and caring for others.

Give students a chance to briefly discuss. You might point out that being created in God's image is a great honor, and it means we have incredible potential to be good and noble persons.

"God sure loves others, doesn't he?"

"And we're made to be like him. That makes what comes next pretty bad."

CHAPTER 2: REBELLION

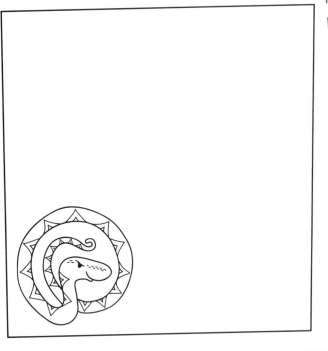

Was she loving God? Or was she being selfish, thinking about what she could get for herself?

She was being selfish and thinking about what she could get.

In the passage above, circle the words that tell what selfish, sinful people deserve.

They deserve the wrath of God.

Now you may be asking, "Why do I get punished for something someone else did? That's SOOOOO not fair!" But sadly, the sin Adam did and the evil that took over his heart is spread to every person, including you.

The first man and woman, Adam and Eve, lived in God's perfect world. But the devil came (as a serpent) and tempted them to eat from the one tree God had commanded them not to eat from. They disobeyed God.

Their selfish rebellion made them God's enemies. It doomed them to live apart from God and to die that way, with sinful and evil hearts. They deserved for God to destroy them.

When the woman saw that the tree was good for food, and that it was a delight to the eyes, and that the tree was to be desired to make one wise, she took of its fruit and ate, and also gave some to her husband who was with her, and he ate. (Genesis 3:6)

The wrath of God is revealed from heaven against all ungodliness and unrighteousness of men. (Romans 1:18)

God had told Adam and Eve not to eat the fruit. Underline the three reasons why Eve decided to eat it anyway.

Sin came into the world through one man, and death through sin, and so death spread to all men because all sinned. (Romans 5:12)

No one does good, not even one. (Romans 3:12)

So add to the picture above to show that you've been selfish and sinned too. Draw a picture of yourself in the picture. Then fill in the blanks below.

Don't forget to add those self-pictures to the Bible story picture!

"I am a

<u>sinner</u>   ,

just like Adam and Eve. I deserve

<u>death / wrath of God</u>

as a punishment."

TALK ABOUT IT

What do you think of how Adam's sin spread to everyone, including you? Do you sense this is true of you? Does it seem right and fair?

Listen to students and let them share their thoughts. If some of them have a problem with the fairness of this, you might point out that:

They sin too, so they too deserve punishment.

Given how they know their own hearts, do they really think they would have chosen any differently than Adam and Eve did?

If fairness were the only issue, Jesus never would have taken the punishment they deserve. God is loving too. They have no reason to fear punishment if they trust him. And if they don't—well, then they're not living as people created in God's image ought to live, and it is fair for them to be punished.

OPTIONAL STOPPING POINT

If you're stopping the lesson here for today, send your students home with *something to think about* and *prayer*.

SOMETHING TO THINK ABOUT

Ending at this point may leave your students asking: "What? Why am I going to be punished for something someone else did? That's not fair!" Help your students see that they are part of the fall. Just like Adam and Eve, they too struggle with selfishness and disobedience.

Tell students: This week, notice examples of how you are selfish and disobedient just like Adam and Eve were. Be ready to give an example at the start of class next time. If you're keeping a journal, write down some of those examples as you notice them.

PRAYER

The entire Bible story including our creation and redemption centers on God's glory. We were originally created for God's glory, in God's own image, but sin has ruined that image. Pray with your students that God would give all of you a desire to reflect God's image and his glory (2 Corinthians 3:18). Ask that he will help you and your students think through areas you struggle with selfishness and disobedience.

When you restart this lesson later, begin with *review*.

REVIEW

Ask students to summarize what happened in each of the first two "chapters" of this lesson's story.

Chapter 1: *God's Perfect World.* *God created a sinless world and made people in his image. Already then, God had chosen believers to be created in the likeness of Jesus to glorify God and enjoy him forever.*

Chapter 2: *Rebellion.* *Mankind disobeyed God and become his enemies, deserving punishment. In Adam, we have all sinned.*

Ask students to share an example of how they too have been selfish or disobedient this week. You may also ask: How has this hurt your relationship with someone else?

CHAPTER 3: THE GOSPEL

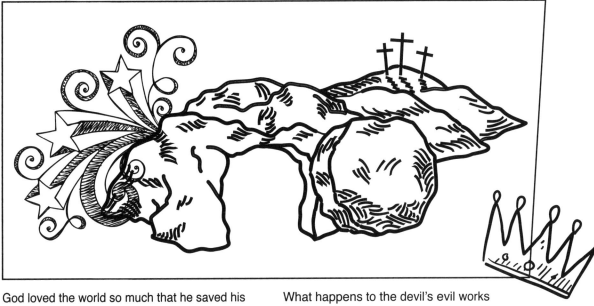

God loved the world so much that he saved his enemies. The Son, Jesus, became a human being. He obeyed the Father perfectly, but took the horrible punishment guilty people deserve. Jesus was nailed to a cross to bleed and die in a shameful and cursed way. On that cross, he died in place of everyone who believes in him.

Jesus was buried, but came back to life in victory! Now the devil is doomed. Jesus rules from heaven and will return one day to judge all people and to live forever with those who believe.

> *For God so loved the world, that he gave his only Son, that whoever believes in him should not perish but have eternal life. (John 3:16)*
>
> *Christ also suffered once for sins, the righteous for the unrighteous, that he might bring us to God. (1 Peter 3:18)*
>
> *The reason the Son of God appeared was to destroy the works of the devil. (1 John 3:8)*

In these verses, underline all the amazing, good things that come to sinners who believe in Jesus.

We do not perish. We have eternal life. We are brought to God.

What happens to the devil's evil works because of Jesus?

They are destroyed.

Here's the best part of the story, the part where you are rescued from death—yes, death! If you believe in Jesus, you are *joined to him* forever. He died—so your sin died too! He came alive—so you do too! He's with God in heaven—so you will be also!

> *We know that our old self was crucified with him in order that the body of sin might be brought to nothing, so that we would no longer be enslaved to sin. (Romans 6:5–6)*
>
> *[God] raised us up with him and seated us with him in the heavenly places in Christ Jesus (Ephesians 2:6).*

So draw a picture of yourself in the picture of the cross and empty tomb. Know that you are part of this story! You're joined to Jesus. The stuck-in-sin person you used to be is dead. Jesus has given you a new life that lets you love God, and one day he will give you a new, never-dying body too. Now fill in the blanks below.

"My old self was *crucified* with Jesus, so I'm not trapped in sin anymore.

God has *raised* me to new life with Jesus."

TALK ABOUT IT

Have you ever thought about these things before:

❑ That when Jesus died, you died too
(in a way)?

❑ That when Jesus rose from the dead, you
became alive too (in a way)?

❑ That as Jesus rules from heaven, you're with him
there (in a way)?

How might knowing you're *that closely* joined to
Jesus change how you think and act?

*Union with Christ is a mystery that's hard to fully
understand. Still, let students talk about this and
assure them that, in a very real sense, believers are
crucified with Jesus, raised with him, and seated
with him in heaven.*

"THAT IS GOOD NEWS!"

"So we all sinned because of Adam, but we have new life because of Jesus."

CHAPTER 4: YOUR LIFE TODAY

Now believers are no longer God's enemies. Instead, they're his dearly loved children. God has given them salvation and changed their hearts. They look to Jesus as they live in this world, knowing they have a mighty Father who will help them when they struggle with selfishness and sin. They learn to love, like their Father, as they wait for Jesus's return.

> *For the grace of God has appeared, bringing salvation for all people, training us to renounce ungodliness and worldly passions, and to live self-controlled, upright, and godly lives in the present age. (Titus 2:11–12)*

In these verses, our salvation (being saved) is called "grace." That means we didn't earn it and don't deserve it. We got it from Jesus. What two things does God's grace teach us to renounce (give up)?

Ungodliness _____

Worldly passions _____

What are three words that describe believers' lives when they know God's grace?

Self-controlled _____

Upright _____

Godly _____

This time, draw the entire picture of yourself in the story. Think of a time when you were tempted to do something wrong—something disobedient, dishonest, or selfish. <u>Draw a picture of yourself saying "no" to that sin, like a believer should, or draw a picture of yourself loving someone else the way Jesus has loved you.</u> That's your life today if you believe in Jesus! YOU are still part of the story.

Students need to have in mind a specific temptation they face and say "no" to. Encourage them that every time they decide to live for God, they are living out their connection to Jesus. They're filling the role God created them to have in the great story. "For we are his workmanship, created in Christ Jesus for good works, which God prepared beforehand, that we should walk in them" (Ephesians 2:10).

SHARING OPPORTUNITY: Be sure to participate by drawing a picture of one of your own temptations and sharing it with your students. Let them see how you, too, are constantly tempted and have an ongoing need to renounce sin and worldly passions. Share how good it feels to act as a believer who's joined to Jesus should act.

As children of God who are joined to Jesus, the Bible tells us to "consider yourselves dead to sin and alive in Christ Jesus" (Romans 6:11). Being joined to Jesus means *we keep dying every day!* Some ways you might "die" to sin and selfishness are:

You give up trying to get your own way all the time. Example from your life:

_____

_____

You give up insisting you be first. Example from your life:_____

_____

_____

You stop complaining when you have to obey someone else. Example from your life:

_____

_____

You love your neighbor like you love yourself. Example from your life: _____

_____

_____

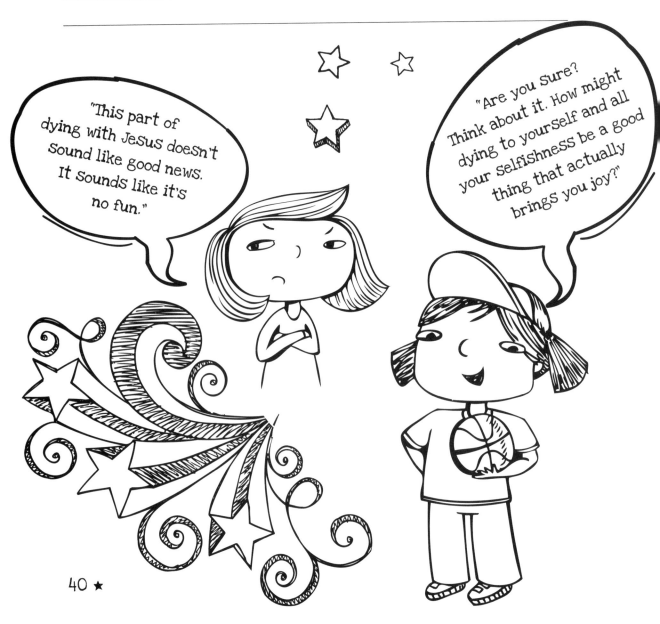

"This part of dying with Jesus doesn't sound like good news. It sounds like it's no fun."

"Are you sure? Think about it. How might dying to yourself and all your selfishness be a good thing that actually brings you joy?"

TALK ABOUT IT

From the list above, pick one or two ways you might die to yourself. On the lines, write examples from your life of how you would do that. Share what you wrote with the group.

Doing those things feels hard, doesn't it? It sounds like death! Well, *of course it does.* But discuss how becoming less concerned about yourself might also be sweet. How might it give you deeper joy? How might dying to yourself also be the way to a new, greater, sweeter life?

This may be a difficult question for some students. Give them plenty of time to think about it. The question will be most helpful to them if it forces them to think about how their constant preoccupation with self is burdensome and makes them slaves to selfishness—and if they see this for themselves. If necessary, you might suggest:

★ *It's freeing to let go of selfishness.*

★ *When you live for yourself, your happiness depends on always getting what you want, and it becomes a burden. When you live for Jesus, your happiness depends on something better—on him!*

★ *A selfless person is wonderfully attractive to God and others. How glorious it is to be such an attractive person!*

★ *A life lived for God and others is purposeful and noble compared to the pettiness of a life lived for self.*

★ *Dying to self is part of being joined to Jesus. Think about it; you're forever connected to the most perfect, glorious person in the universe. Don't you want to live that life?*

Help students see that dying to self is a sweet part of being joined to Jesus—and part of God's good news for us.

Close your discussion with prayer. You and your students who profess to be believers might thank your Father for how you're joined to Jesus, and ask him to help you live in ways that fit the dearly loved children you are.

MAKE IT STICK:

WATCH YOUR WORDS

(Take 5 minutes at the end of the session to explain the coming week's "Make It Stick" exercise.)

INSTRUCTIONS:

❑ Fill out this Make It Stick page during the week.

The gospel tells us that Jesus makes us good in God's eyes. Believing this should help us no longer feel a need to make ourselves look good to others, either by bragging about ourselves or putting other people down. James 3:2 says, "If anyone does not stumble in what he says, he is a perfect man."

This week, practice living like God's child by watching your words (what you say).
For one week, or until the next time you meet, do not:

- Lie

- Say unkind things about others (gossip)

- Put anyone down

- Complain

- Brag

- Hide your sin

- Make excuses

- Defend yourself (even if you're wrongly accused)

If you like, you can keep notes about how you're doing on the bottom part or back of this page.

Your students may protest that some of the behaviors forbidden in the Watch Your Words assignment aren't necessarily sinful. For example, defending oneself is sometimes a good thing. Explain that this is true. Defending oneself isn't always inherently sinful. But the reason we're usually so quick to defend ourselves is our desire to look good to others, which is opposed to gospel faith and to believing that Jesus has already made us righteous in God's eyes. For this exercise, we're practicing control of that desire. This is why our goal is to refrain from all these tongue behaviors, whether they're inherently sinful or not.

_____

_____

_____

_____

MY TONGUE IS CONNECTED TO MY—WHAT?
Big Idea: Sin of the Heart

NOTES TO THE LEADER

LESSON GOAL

Using their experience with sins of the tongue, students will understand that the sins they do come from sin they love in their hearts—and that they need God's help to renew their hearts.

SUMMARY

This lesson will begin with an essential discussion of how you and your students did with the Watch Your Words assignment from last time. The point of this discussion is for them to see their helplessness in the face of sin and their need for Jesus. The discussion will also start your group thinking about how sin proceeds from the heart. The lesson is built around four things your students might want to say as they study this topic.

1. **"I want to look right!"** *The desire to look right to others is deeply engrained. It's the motive behind much lying, bragging, gossiping, complaining, and excuse-making. Your students will match outward sins with the I-want-to-look-right motives behind them.*

2. **"Don't blame me!"** *In contrast to the righteousness God gives us by faith in Jesus, self-justification is our own attempt to look right. Your students will look at examples from the Bible of how self-justification leads to blame-shifting and excuse-making, and will share examples of this from their own lives.*

3. **"I'm not so bad deep down . . . am I?"** *Evil sins and attitudes come from the heart. Your students will take a closer look at their attitudes toward the Watch Your Words assignment to see what's happening in their hearts.*

4. **"So what hope do I have?"** *Although all this may sound like bad news, it's actually part of the good news—the gospel. Your students will learn that the hopelessness of their sin should drive them to Jesus, who alone is able to mend hearts. You and they will practice faith in Jesus by praying for heart-level renewal.*

YOUR PREPARATION

STUDY. Read through the lesson and teaching notes. Make sure you're familiar with the following Bible passages and can answer questions your students may have about them:

★ *God's confrontation with Adam and Eve in Genesis 3.*

★ *Aaron's sin with the golden calf in Exodus 32.*

Jesus's discussion about godly behavior and the heart from Luke 6:37–49.

BE READY TO SHARE. Sharing your personal stories is always important, and it's doubly important in this lesson. This is the first time you'll be asking students to share deeply about their sin. They may feel they can't be that open. This means it's essential that you show them it's safe for God's children to admit their sin—by readily admitting examples of your own sin. Make your examples specific, not vague. How honestly you do this will likely make a big difference in how open your students feel they can be about their sin for the rest of the entire course. You'll have two particular opportunities:

1. *You'll need to share at the very start of the session, when you review how everyone did on the Watch Your Words assignment. Be ready with specific examples, including your failures.*

2. *An example from your life of blame-shifting or excuse-making. You'll need not only to share an example, but also to explain how you were trying to justify yourself.*

PRAY. Ask God to give your students godly conviction of their sin that readies them for repentance. Such conviction is a grace of God, and you need to pray for it for your students. Without such conviction, the lesson you're about to lead may merely make your students feel condemned or hounded by you or by God.

BEFORE YOU BEGIN

(About 15 minutes)

Talk about the Watch Your Words assignment from last time. How well did you do? What parts of it were the hardest? List or discuss some of the ways you struggled.

Help students discuss the difficulty of keeping the Watch Your Words assignment. Give them plenty of time to share stories of how they tried. If any students think they were successful in keeping the assignment, question them and gently show them how none of us keeps it perfectly.

SHARING OPPORTUNITY: Be sure to share several examples of how you, too, did the Watch Your Words assignment and failed to keep it very well. The entire What's Up? course depends on students feeling free to share openly about their sin and their struggles. Set a tone of openness about sin now—by admitting specific examples of your own sin and your failure with the Watch Your Words assignment.

IMPORTANT: The goal of the Watch Your Words assignment is to help students see their need for Jesus. Therefore, there are things this opening discussion must NOT become:

- ★ *DON'T let it become a discussion comparing how well students did in keeping the Watch Your Words assignment.*

- ★ *DON'T let it become a platform for urging kids to try harder or do better in controlling their tongues (even though they should do better, that's not your purpose right now).*

INSTEAD, your goal must be to help students see that they're desperate sinners who are unable to keep God's law simply by trying hard in their own strength. The power to change must come from God. Help students to see that the Watch Your Words assignment convicts them of their sin—meaning they need Jesus!

Remember some things you learned last time:

- Being joined to Jesus makes you a child of God, so you can love him and obey him gladly—even in how you use your tongue.

- Your old self was crucified with Jesus, so you're not trapped in sin anymore.

However, trying to do the Watch Your Words assignment under your own power might make you *feel* like you're still trapped in sin.

When you were doing the Watch Your Words assignment, did you think to believe the gospel—that God loves you as his child? Did you pray to your Father and trust him to help you keep from sinning? Or did you try to keep the assignment in your own power?

Remind students that we fight sin by trusting God, and gently tell them that this takes practice. There will be many failures. These help us learn to trust more and more in God rather than in ourselves. Encourage them that God is determined to see them grow and conquer sin in their lives.

TODAY'S LESSON

Did you know that your tongue is one of the hardest working organs in your body? Not only is your tongue busy talking, mixing food, swallowing, fighting germs, and keeping you from drooling on your pillow at night—it also shows what's in your heart.

The Bible says the tongue can deceive, lie, gossip, slander, and speak hatred. It can also speak wisdom, kindness, gentleness, truth, and worship. The tongue is powerful! And the things we say with our tongue show us our need for the gospel every day (even every minute).

In this lesson, you'll learn how the things you *say* with your tongue show what you *love* in your heart. The lesson has four steps. They're based on four things you might want to say along the way:

- "I want to look right!"

- "Don't blame me!"

- "I'm not so bad deep down . . . am I?"

- "So what hope do I have?"

"I WANT TO LOOK RIGHT!"
(About 15 minutes)

You may never be tempted to steal. You may not struggle with cheating on a test. So why is controlling your tongue different? Why was the Watch Your Words assignment SO HARD?

Read Matthew 6:1. Fill in the blanks to see something all of us naturally want—but Jesus said we should beware of.

"Beware of practicing your *righteousness* _____ before other

people in order to be *seen by them* _____" (Matthew 6:1).

Controlling your tongue is so hard because we want to look right to other people. We want others to think we're . . .

good . . .

or smart . . .

or fun to be with.

We want this SO MUCH that we'll sin with our tongues to try to make it happen. We'll lie and brag and say bad things about others.

Let's look at how we try to make ourselves look right to others. Match each behavior from the Watch Your Words assignment with the I-want-to-look-right *motives* for doing them. Write the tongue behavior beneath the motive. (Some behaviors might fit more than one motive.)

| 1. Lying | 2. Gossiping | 3. Putting people down | 4. Making excuses |
| 5. Bragging | 6. Complaining | 7. Defending yourself | 8. Hiding your sin |

"I'm sure to point out anything I do right in case others missed it. I whine if they don't agree."

"I make other people look bad so I'll look better."

"When I'm wrong, I try to keep anyone from noticing or I make up a story about being right."

"I can't handle it when others think I'm wrong, so I always correct them."

First example: bragging, complaining. Second example: gossiping, putting people down. Third example: lying, hiding your sin. Fourth example: defending yourself, making excuses.

It's not important that students match the examples with the motives exactly this way. The point is for them to see that the underlying urge in much of their tongue sin is to get others to think well of them. Help them to understand that the urge to make ourselves look right is the "sin under the sin."

TALK ABOUT IT

Now tell about how *you* want to look right to other people. What are some places and times in your life when looking right to others feels especially important to you? Give an example of how you sometimes sin with your tongue to try to make yourself look right in those situations.

You may have to help students think of situations by suggesting some categories: are they more concerned with looking right in front of their friends, at school, at home, or at church?

SHARING OPPORTUNITY: Be prepared to get the conversation started by sharing one of your own struggles in this area. Tell of a situation in which you feel pressure to make yourself look right and how you're tempted to sin to make that happen. Urge students to share the same, and when they do, make sure your tone is an understanding one, not a scolding one. If you feel the need, point them to Jesus as the only source of the true righteousness from God that satisfies our thirst to be right. Lesson 4 will deal with that concept in depth, but it's okay to introduce that good news now if you sense your students need to hear it.

"DON'T BLAME ME!"
(About 15 minutes)

God makes us right in his eyes when we have faith in Jesus. That's the kind of "being right" we really need! Wanting to make ourselves *look* right to others is the wrong kind of "being right." It's called "self-justification."

Self-justification: Trying to make yourself look right or not guilty.

Self-justification happens *very* easily. It's like a reflex—like how you hold up your hand to protect yourself if you're about to be hit. In the same way, when we're caught doing wrong our reflex action is to deny it or blame someone else (even if that hurts the other person!).

Let's look at some examples in the Bible.

Look up and read: Genesis 3:8–12. It's about when Adam and Eve were caught disobeying God.

When Adam was caught doing wrong, did he admit his sin or try to make excuses and blame someone else?

He made excuses and shifted blame.

Who did he blame?

Eve, and God indirectly—"the woman you made"

Look up and read: Exodus 32:21–24. It's about when Moses caught Aaron in sin after Aaron made a golden calf for the people to worship.

When Aaron was caught doing wrong, did he admit his sin or try to make excuses and blame someone else?

He made excuses and shifted blame.

Who did he blame?

The people

What excuses, and even lies, did he come up with?

The people were pushy. The calf just came out of the fire.

TALK ABOUT IT

Now think of a time (either during the Watch Your Words assignment or some other time) when you were caught doing wrong and made excuses or blamed someone else. Tell about it. How were you trying to make yourself look right instead of admitting your sin?

SHARING OPPORTUNITY: Here again, you may need to lead off with an example of blame-shifting or excuse-making from your own life. Be sure to include how you wanted others to think you were more right than you really were.

OPTIONAL STOPPING POINT

If you're stopping the lesson here for today, send your students home with *something to think about* and *prayer*.

SOMETHING TO THINK ABOUT

Tell students: Before you leave, write on a piece of paper what you think is your favorite way of using your tongue to make others think you're better than you really are. It might be:

- ★ *Lying*
- ★ *Bragging*
- ★ *Criticizing*
- ★ *Making excuses*
- ★ *Blaming others*
- ★ *Gossiping*

Then fold up the paper and take it with you. Try to remember to carry it around with you in the coming week (like in a pocket—but don't let it go through the wash!). Then whenever you notice it, remind yourself that you don't need to make yourself look right.

PRAYER

Pray with your students that God would show you and them way in which you try to justify sinful behavior by making excuses and blame-shifting. Encourage your students to remember that Jesus came for sinners (all of us). Jesus works in the lives of sinners who repent and put their faith in him. Being joined to Jesus makes you a child of God, even when you sin. Thank him for this in your prayer.

When you restart this lesson later, begin with *review*.

REVIEW

Ask students: Do you remember what self-justification is? (Trying to make yourself look right or not guilty.) Remind students of the lesson's first two main points about self-justification:

"I want to look right!" *The desire to look right to others is deeply engrained. It's the motive behind much lying, bragging, gossiping, complaining and excuse-making.*

"Don't blame me!" *We hate to admit our sin and will blame others to get around it.*

Ask: Did you notice yourself doing that this week? Invite students to share examples, or share one about yourself.

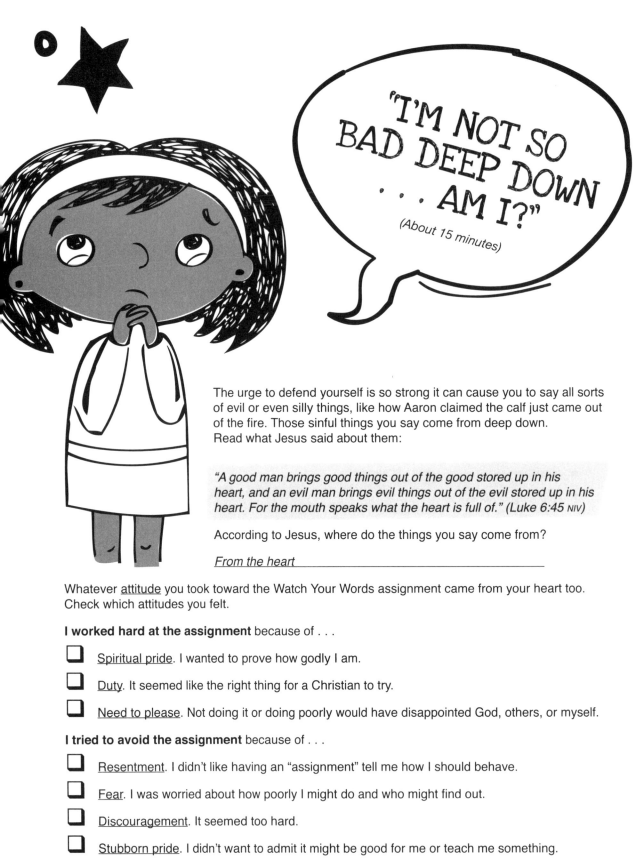

"I'M NOT SO BAD DEEP DOWN . . . AM I?"

(About 15 minutes)

The urge to defend yourself is so strong it can cause you to say all sorts of evil or even silly things, like how Aaron claimed the calf just came out of the fire. Those sinful things you say come from deep down. Read what Jesus said about them:

"A good man brings good things out of the good stored up in his heart, and an evil man brings evil things out of the evil stored up in his heart. For the mouth speaks what the heart is full of." (Luke 6:45 NIV)

According to Jesus, where do the things you say come from?

From the heart

Whatever <u>attitude</u> you took toward the Watch Your Words assignment came from your heart too. Check which attitudes you felt.

I worked hard at the assignment because of . . .

❑ <u>Spiritual pride</u>. I wanted to prove how godly I am.

❑ <u>Duty</u>. It seemed like the right thing for a Christian to try.

❑ <u>Need to please</u>. Not doing it or doing poorly would have disappointed God, others, or myself.

I tried to avoid the assignment because of . . .

❑ <u>Resentment</u>. I didn't like having an "assignment" tell me how I should behave.

❑ <u>Fear</u>. I was worried about how poorly I might do and who might find out.

❑ <u>Discouragement</u>. It seemed too hard.

❑ <u>Stubborn pride</u>. I didn't want to admit it might be good for me or teach me something.

I mostly ignored the assignment or forgot about it because of . . .

❑ <u>Not caring</u>. Other things were more on my mind.

❑ <u>Coldness</u>. Living in a godly way just doesn't get me excited or hold my interest.

TALK ABOUT IT

Discuss the attitudes you checked. What has the Watch Your Words assignment taught you about your sin? How deep does the sin go?

Help students understand that heart attitudes affect all we do and are the underlying cause of our individual sins. Students who worked hard at the assignment should not necessarily feel they're less sinful than those who didn't, since they may have done so out of pride or a desire to show off.

It's a big step for students to be able to see and admit their underlying attitudes and motivations. Some might resist sharing. But it's important that they begin to be open and honest about their sin. As a leader, you can help them by being ready and willing to share your own underlying, sinful motivations.

"SO WHAT HOPE DO I HAVE?"

(30 minutes)

Let's review. Think of and list three things you've learned in this lesson about how you sin with your tongue.

_____

_____

_____

_____

Allow students to ponder the question and come up with answers. After listening to and affirming their answers, point them to the three main points made in this lesson so far. You may want to write them down on a whiteboard.

Your sin shows that inside you're selfish, wanting others to think you're right.

Your sin hurts others as well as you. You're quick to use your words to blame other people.

Your sin isn't just that you slip up sometimes. The evil things you say come from evil desires in your heart.

You might think this sounds like horribly **BAD NEWS!**

But it's actually part of the **GOOD NEWS**—the gospel. These are three reasons why you need Jesus!

By now you should realize that <u>you're a far worse sinner than you ever thought</u>. This means you can give up trying to fight your sin by yourself. It'll never work. Trust Jesus instead. Only Jesus can change a sinful heart!

 Point to remember:
When you fight to not sin, don't try to do it by yourself.
Do it by trusting God.

No matter how yucky your sin is (and it's VERY yucky!), God forgives you when you believe in Jesus. And no matter how much evil is in your heart, God still loves you and helps your heart change.

A godly king named David wrote Psalm 139. It's a prayer in the Bible. David understood how God knew all his secret sins yet loved him anyway. Here's part of the prayer he wrote:

Search me, God, and know my heart; test me and know my anxious thoughts. See if there is any offensive way in me, and lead me in the way everlasting. (Psalm 139:23–24 NIV)

David's prayer asks God for six things. Find them and list them below.

1. *Search me*

2. *Know my heart*

3. *Test me*

4. *Know my anxious thoughts*

5. *See my offensive ways*

6. *Lead me in a better, godly way*

Look at the list. First <u>underline</u> any words that mention something that gets in the way of enjoying God.

Now put a star next to every request that invites God to know or see something about us—even our sin!

Now add another star next to the part that asks God to change us.

PRAY ABOUT IT

Finally, make David's prayer your prayer too. Trust God and invite him to know the truth about your heart and to change you. Have each person in the group pick two of the requests that have stars next to them. Take turns praying that God would do those things in your life, or write out your prayer below.

This lesson has likely been a convicting one, and so it's essential that students end by turning to God in faith. Encourage them that no sin is too big for him to forgive and no life is too sinful for him to redeem. Encourage them to habitually look to God for both assurance of forgiveness and help in fighting sin.

If you find your group finishing early, don't hesitate to pray more. You might decide to break the group into smaller groups or pairs and have students pray about the specific sins they mentioned earlier in this lesson. Taking our sin to God for him to deal with (both in forgiving us and helping us overcome it) is an excellent habit to practice!

MAKE IT STICK:

WATCH YOUR WORDS (PART 2)

(Take 5 minutes at the end of the session to explain the coming week's "Make It Stick" exercise.)

INSTRUCTIONS:

❑ Fill out this Make It Stick page during the week

The Watch Your Words assignment was hard, wasn't it? Well, God is so holy and good that his commands about the tongue are actually *even harder* than that. It isn't enough to AVOID saying bad or selfish things. There are also good and kind things we DO say.

Ephesians 4:29 (NIV) says, "Do not let any unwholesome talk come out of your mouths, but only what is helpful for building others up according to their needs, that it may benefit whose who listen."

This week, focus on what you DO say. Talk in ways that benefit others. Instead of trying to make yourself look good, admit your mistakes and confess your sin. Instead of bragging about yourself, talk lots about how good others are. Especially, talk lots about the goodness of Jesus.

Until the next time you meet, do the following:

- Admit your mistakes

- Confess your sin to others

- Tell others you're sorry when you hurt them (and mean it!)

- Encourage others (this includes not getting jealous if they do something better than you, but instead congratulating them)

- Give good reports about others

- Tell others about Jesus

Again, you can keep notes on this page if you like.

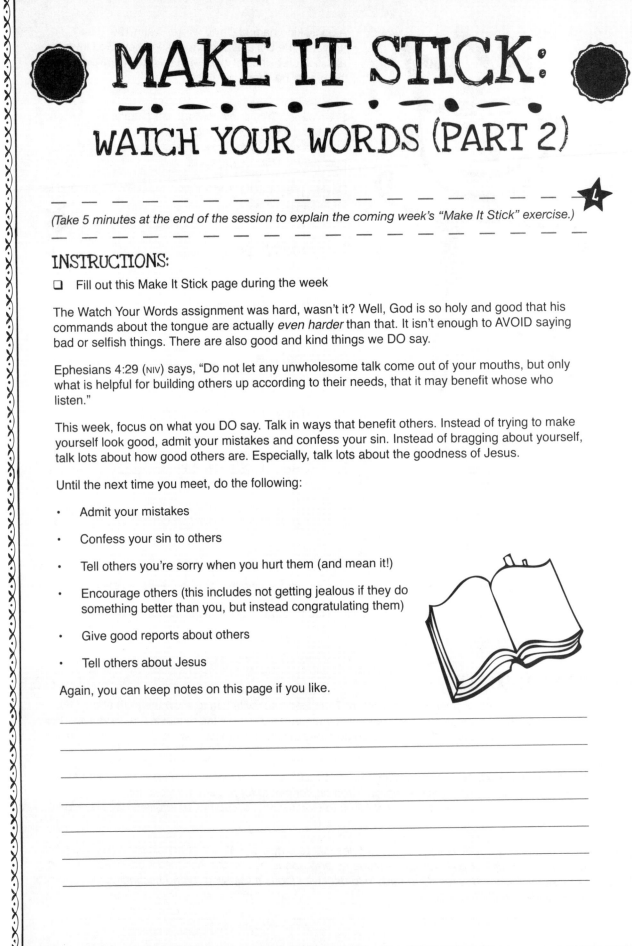

_____

_____

_____

_____

_____

_____

_____

HMM...WHAT GRADES DO I GET?

Big Idea: Justification by Faith

NOTES TO THE LEADER

This lesson has no optional stopping point and should not be divided. If you have a short class period and normally divide lessons into two sessions, you may need to work through this lesson a bit more quickly than usual to get through it in time. If you have a long class period, use the optional discussion questions in this lesson to spend more time discussing justification with your students.

LESSON GOAL

Students will learn the difference between self-justification and the justification by faith that God gives in Jesus. They will be encouraged to put their faith in Jesus—either for the first time or more deeply than before.

SUMMARY

Last time, students learned about the dangers of self-justification. In this lesson, they'll learn about the better kind of justification that isn't earned but rather is given by God. The lesson uses two main teaching tools: 1) Jesus's parable of the Pharisee and the tax collector, and 2) an illustration of a report card.

The Pharisee/tax collector parable shows our urge to justify ourselves before God, and how that doesn't work. Your students will learn how the Pharisee worked hard to obey God but still felt a need to prove himself—and went home without being justified.

The report card illustration will show a better way to be justified; God's way. Your students will give themselves grades in spiritual "subjects," like telling the truth. The lesson will walk them through the following process:

★ They'll recognize that whatever grades they've earned aren't good enough for God.

★ They'll see how some of the wrong ways people sometimes think about becoming right with God are not good enough.

★ They'll see how only in Jesus they are given a righteousness they could never earn.

The lesson ends with an opportunity to practice greater faith in Jesus through prayer. Students who haven't yet begun a life of faith may be encouraged to do so. Students who already practice faith will be called to make that faith stronger and deeper.

YOUR PREPARATION

STUDY. Read through the lesson and become thoroughly familiar beforehand with the report card illustration and the concept it intends to teach. The report card demonstrates the exchange enjoyed by those who are in Christ—how he takes the consequences for our sin (even though he didn't deserve that) and we receive the righteousness that's his (even though we haven't earned it). Be sure you're clear on the following points:

★ Believers have earned NOTHING by their efforts to obey God, no matter how successful they seem to have been.

★ Believers are credited with PERFECT RIGHTEOUSNESS through faith in Jesus, no matter how much they may still fail to obey God.

★ Pay attention to the terms you use when talking about the report card illustration. It's about what we've earned (nothing but Fs) and what we're given (all As)—what in theological terms is called "justification." The lesson uses the terms "earned" and "given." You should try to do so too, because it helps make a distinction between justification and growth as a Christian—called "sanctification." In Christian growth, there is a sense in which one might have "middle grades" or show improvement. If your students ask, be clear that this lesson is not about such growth but rather about what we've earned.

BEFORE YOU BEGIN
(About 10 minutes)

How did you do with the second part of the Watch Your Words assignment? This time, give yourself a grade (from A to F) on how well you controlled your tongue in each of these areas:

ASSIGNMENT	GRADE
Admitted your mistakes (without being asked)	--------------
Confessed your sin to others	--------------
Told others you were sorry when you hurt them	--------------
Encouraged others and congratulated them when they did better than you	--------------
Gave good reports about others	--------------
Told others about Jesus	--------------

Discuss the grades you gave yourself and share some examples of what you did to deserve your grades.

Use the grades at this point only to get the students talking and sharing. Resist the urge to comment on what grades you think would be appropriate. Accept whatever grade the student believes he or she earned.

TODAY'S LESSON
(About 40 minutes, more with the optional discussion questions)

Last time, you learned how tempting it is to try *self-justification*.
Find the definition of self-justification from the last lesson and write it here:

Trying to make yourself look right or not guilty

Today's lesson is about how you can look right <u>to God</u>. Instead of self-justification, you'll learn about a better kind of justification that comes from God. It's called *justification by faith*.

"WHAT'S SO BAD ABOUT TRYING TO PROVE TO GOD HOW GOOD I AM?"

One day Jesus told a story to a crowd of self-justifiers. The story was about two men. First learn about the characters in his story:

Pharisee

Respected member of a synagogue (like a church)

Worked hard at carefully obeying God's laws

Known by all to be a good person

Tax Collector

Traitor who worked for the Romans—the enemy!

Got rich by taking other people's money

Known by all to be a bad person

Now read Jesus's story in **Luke 18:9–14**.

Pick and write two things the Pharisee told God about himself.

One bad thing he was NOT: _____

One good thing he did: _____

Do you see? The Pharisee was a good person in many ways, but he was still wrong because he was trying to justify himself before God! He was trying to make himself look right and not guilty to God. That never works if you really want to be *justified*.

 Justification: When God says he counts you righteous, not guilty.

"SO IF JUSTIFICATION COMES FROM GOD, HOW DO I GET IT?"

Let's start with how good or bad you are. Give yourself grades again. This time, imagine God keeps a report card on *all* your behavior— not just "tongue" behaviors. Put your name on the report card. Then fill in the grades you think your life has earned from God, from A to F. Try to be honest.

Report Card

Telling the truth ☐

Encouraging others ☐

Obeying parents ☐

Being generous ☐

Putting others first ☐

Name:

TALK ABOUT IT

Now discuss the grades you gave yourself. What have you done to earn them? Do you think you're doing okay, or are you concerned that your grades aren't better?

There are no "right answers" at this point. Simply encourage students to share what they think.

If you're either proud of your grades or worried about them, it means you're trusting *yourself* instead of Jesus. You're a self-justifier.

OPTIONAL DISCUSSION FOR LONGER CLASS SESSIONS: If you have a long class period, take time here for further discussion about pride and worry. Write the following two descriptions on a whiteboard:

★ *PRIDE: I like to show off my good Christian performance.*

★ *WORRY: I'm discouraged because I think God is upset with me over my failures.*

Ask students: Which statement is most true of you? Which is worse?

Allow for discussion and sharing. Help students to see that both pride and worry are forms of self-justification. Both come from trusting yourself and how well you do rather than trusting Jesus.

The next step is to remember that the gospel says you're a very big sinner—much worse than you thought. Consider these verses:

> *"You therefore must be perfect, as your heavenly Father is perfect."*
> (Matthew 5:48)
>
> *"None is righteous, no, not one; no one understands; no one seeks for God."*
> (Romans 3:10–11)
>
> *We have all become like one who is unclean, and all our righteous deeds like a polluted garment. (Isaiah 64:6)*

Things you do that seem right and good might mean you're making progress in your spiritual life. But according to the verses above, are they ever good enough to *earn* anything from God?

No

Report Card

Telling the truth ☐

Encouraging others ☐

Obeying parents ☐

Being generous ☐

Putting others first ☐

Name:

In school, you get an okay grade even if your work is not perfect. But God is so holy that he demands PERFECT grades! With God, anything not absolutely perfect earns an F.

Adjust your report card to fit the way God sees your attempts to impress him by yourself. Write your name on it again. This time give yourself all Fs. That's the only grade you've *earned* from God.

Make sure each student fills out a report card filled with Fs. Make sure you fill out a report card with Fs for yourself, too, so that your students see that you too admit that your sin is horrible in God's sight and you've only earned Fs.

"HOW CAN I IMPROVE MY GRADES WITH GOD?"

Having all Fs with God is a big problem because he demands straight A's. You need to become right with God. You need a report card full of A's.

Here are some possible solutions. Notice how each one actually doesn't work.

1. THE "A FOR EFFORT" SOLUTION:

"If I try real hard to be good, God might decide trying was good enough."

"WON'T WORK. You'll end up awfully discouraged and worried. You'll soon realize you can never try hard enough."

Quickly draw a worried face here.

2. THE "FORGIVENESS ONLY" SOLUTION:

"God forgives, doesn't he? I can ask him to just erase all my FS."

"WON'T WORK. That isn't good enough. You'll be left with just a blank report card. Your Christian life will feel like a burden as you try to earn some As to get God to not just forgive you, but actually like you."

Draw a frustrated face here.

3. THE "CREDIT FOR NOTHING" SOLUTION:

"WON'T WORK. What good is an A that hasn't been earned? You'll never appreciate it because it's so cheap."

"God can just give me all AS. He's nice and he can do anything."

Draw an I-don't-care face here.

Which false solution is most like the way you sometimes think about your sin problem?
Circle 1, 2, or 3. Discuss why these solutions are false ones.

Make sure students notice the dialogue that explains why these solutions are not good enough. Trying hard ends in worry. Forgiveness alone still leaves a burden. Cheap A's are meaningless.

Now here's God's solution for making you right with him. Write your name again on the first report card—the one with all Fs. Now notice there's a second report card. It belongs to Jesus!

The Bible says Jesus "has been tempted as we are, yet without sin" (Hebrews 4:15). Think of all the perfectly good things Jesus did. Then mark Jesus's report card with all A+'s for his good life.

 Justification: what makes one right in God's eyes

Now read some verses that tell us God's solution—how we become *justified* and *right*.

For our sake he made him to be sin who knew no sin, so that in him we might become the righteousness of God. (2 Corinthians 5:21)

Who actually sinned? Circle one		Me	Jesus
But who gets punished for it? Circle one		Me	Jesus
Who actually did right? Circle one		Me	Jesus
But who gets righteousness? Circle one		Me	Jesus

For Christ also suffered once for sins, the righteous for the unrighteous, that he might bring us to God. (1 Peter 3:18)

Who was right, but still suffered?

Jesus

Who was not right, but still gets to be accepted by God?

Me

The righteousness of God has been manifested . . . through faith in Jesus Christ for all who believe . . . and are justified by his grace as a gift. (Romans 3:21–24)

Where do we get this righteousness?

From God

Do we earn it by anything we do?

No

If not, how *do* we get it?

By faith in Jesus. It's a gift of God.

When you belong to Jesus by believing in him, it's like he's traded report cards with you.

❑ <u>Jesus took your sin</u>. By dying on the cross he took the punishment for everything wrong you've ever done or will do. He suffered the anger of God that you deserve and all the shame of being wrong.

❑ <u>God gives you Jesus's right record</u>. God no longer sees you as shameful and wrong. Instead he sees the righteousness of Jesus when he looks at you and all you do. You are forever justified.

Now turn back to the last set of report cards. On Jesus's report card scratch out his name. Write YOUR NAME in its place. This is now *your* report card. Then scratch out your name on the bad report card and write "Jesus" in its place.

TALK ABOUT IT

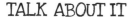

Share how it felt to do this. Were you embarrassed back when you had to give yourself the Fs? How does it feel now to know Jesus took that shame for you?

How does the unearned righteousness God gives you feel different from the kind of right reputation you have to earn?

Becoming right with God doesn't happen because of anything good you do. You get it by placing your **faith** in Jesus. You stop trusting what *you* do and start trusting *him*, instead.

Faith: Believing that Jesus died for your sin and trusting him—not your own good behavior—to make you right with God.

PRAY ABOUT IT

End by saying a prayer.

- ☐ Pray that the Holy Spirit would free you from the need to prove yourself.

- ☐ Pray that he would teach you to trust the perfect righteousness that comes from Jesus, instead.

- ☐ Pray that you'll stop being either proud or worried.

Speak your prayer aloud or write it below.

_____

_____

_____

_____

_____

_____

_____

_____

_____

Be sure to take time to pray here. Prayer is an excellent way to exercise faith in Jesus.

The call to place one's faith in Jesus is for both unbelievers and believers. If some students say they haven't yet put their faith in Jesus and haven't been given As from God, encourage them to turn away from their sin and to start putting their faith in Jesus today. For those students who say they've already begun a life of faith, encourage them to keep practicing that faith and to deepen it. Stronger faith in the righteousness from God that's ours in Jesus defeats pride and worry—and makes for confident, obedient, growing believers.

MAKE IT STICK:

TEACH JUSTIFICATION BY FAITH

(Take 5 minutes at the end of the session to explain the coming week's "Make It Stick" exercise.)

INSTRUCTIONS:

☐ Fill out this Make It Stick page during the week.

☐ If you have time, go ahead and get started now.

Now it's *your* turn to teach someone else how we become right with God. Pick someone and teach it to them before the next time you meet. That's when you'll report to the group on how it went.

You may pick someone who already knows all about justification or someone who doesn't. It's your choice. (Just don't be bossy, like *they* need to hear it. Explain that you're doing it because it helps *you* learn.)

Study first. You can learn about justification from the three verses you read near the end of this lesson: 2 Corinthians 5:21; 1 Peter 3:18; and Romans 3:21–24. When you teach, you may also use the report card illustration if you want. Make sure your teaching includes these five points:

1. We are sinners; we are not right with God.

2. Jesus, who was perfect, took the punishment we deserve.

3. We become right with God by trusting Jesus in faith, not by anything good we do.

4. God says we are right in his eyes and totally accepted. He gives us a perfect righteousness we could never earn.

5. Righteousness from God frees us to live for him out of thankfulness, not out of pride or worry.

TIP #1: It might help to practice first with someone else in your group or at home.

TIP #2: It will also help to first write down in your own words what justification by faith means.

You can do that in the space below or on the back of this page.

_____

_____

_____

_____

If you have the time, breaking students up into pairs to have them practice teaching justification by faith would be an excellent exercise—both good review, and good practice for the assignment.

PRESENTS? FOR ME?!

Big Idea: Holiness and Fighting Sin

NOTES TO THE LEADER

LESSON GOAL

Students will recognize more benefits of being joined to Jesus and will learn to draw on these as they fight to obey God better.

SUMMARY

The past two lessons were about JUSTIFICATION. This lesson will introduce two more benefits of being joined to Jesus by faith:

★ ADOPTION. We become God's dearly loved children, with all the blessings children enjoy.

★ SANCTIFICATION (which we'll call "BECOMING HOLY"). We are new people, made holy and able to live for God by his Spirit.

PART 1 of the lesson will help your students appreciate these benefits. They're like presents from God. Your students will learn about these presents by discussing what makes them so wonderful.

PART 2 takes a closer look at becoming holy. Holiness is an ongoing process in which believers cooperate with God's work in their lives, overcoming sin and resisting the devil. The Bible says to "put on the whole armor of God" (Ephesians 6:11). The armor described is remarkably similar to the benefits of JUSTIFICATION, ADOPTION and BECOMING HOLY. We use all the benefits of being joined to Jesus as we work to become ever more holy! In this section, you and your students will:

Learn that fighting sin is something to do with God, trusting his constant help, not by oneself to impress God.

Learn that two essential weapons in the battle against sin are <u>prayer</u> and the <u>Word of God</u>.

Think about how specific sins can be battled by using prayer, the Word of God and the rest of the "armor."

Practice using the armor by reading a Scripture passage together and praying together for victory over sin.

YOUR PREPARATION

STUDY. Read over the lesson and teaching notes, and become familiar with the discussion of the armor of God in Ephesians 6:10–20. Also, be sure you understand the difference between BECOMING HOLY and the other benefits of being joined to Jesus. JUSTIFICATION and ADOPTION are one-time events completed by God at the moment one becomes a Christian. BECOMING HOLY is a God-worked change that begins immediately too, but it's also a process that continues throughout the Christian life and requires the believer's cooperation. We work—with God, and using all the benefits of being in Christ—at constantly becoming more holy and obeying God better.

BE READY TO SHARE. You'll have two particular opportunities to share stories about your personal battles with sin:

During discussion of the differences between trying to fight sin under one's own power and fighting it by using the strength God gives.

Before and during the closing prayer when you ask God for help in overcoming particular temptations.

PRAY. Pray that both you and your students would be in awe of the presents you've received from God and that a thankful spirit of glad fighting against sin would mark the class time.

BEFORE YOU BEGIN

(15 minutes)

Talk about how it went teaching justification by faith. You should have taught five things:

1. **Sin** – We are not right with God.

2. **Jesus** – He did right, but took the punishment we deserve.

3. **Faith** – We become right with God by faith in Jesus, not by anything good we do.

4. **Righteousness** – God says we are right in his eyes and totally accepted. He gives us a perfect righteousness we could never earn.

5. **Freedom** – The great thing about righteousness from God is it frees us to live for him out of thankfulness, not because we're worried or proud.

Did you do the assignment? If so, did you talk about Jesus happily or did you wish you didn't have to?

Sometimes people get scared to talk about Jesus because . . .

❑ They think they won't say things right, or . . .

❑ It feels too personal, or . . .

❑ They worry what others will think of them.

Did you get scared in any of those ways? Which ones?

When it happened, did you remember that your righteousness comes from Jesus—not how well you do or what others think of you?

Telling someone about Jesus can be an intimidating experience for many students. Use this discussion as an opportunity to show students that the gospel gives confidence. They don't need to worry that God will be disappointed with their efforts because there's no need to impress him. Nor will they worry what others think if their security comes from what God thinks.

Even after students understand this, they may still feel insecure and seek approval from others or try to prove themselves to God. Reassure them that overcoming this takes time—a lifetime!—but deeply believing the gospel will help.

TODAY'S LESSON

Justification is great! But in this lesson you'll learn how it's only the start. God also gives you other, equally stunning gifts when you believe in Jesus—like getting presents. All these presents will make you more confident when you have to do hard things for Jesus (like tell people about him).

PART 1: PRESENTS FROM GOD

(30 minutes)

In this section you'll learn about the presents God gives you.
You'll also think about what makes them great.

REVIEW:

In Lesson 2, you learned that when you believe in Jesus your life is *joined to him*.

❑ Like he was killed, your old sinful life is dead.

❑ Like he was raised to life, you have a new life now.

Think of being joined to Jesus as a birthday—one where you get lots of presents. You might open the first gift and it's *so* good that you think, "Wow! This present has to be the BIG ONE!" But then you open more and find that the other presents are just as awesome.

Now let's learn about three of the great presents believers get from God. The first is one you already know about . . .

GOD'S PRESENT FOR YOU: JUSTIFICATION

Joined to Jesus, your sins are forgiven and you're counted righteous, even though you still sin sometimes.

First, find **Romans 3:23–24** in your Bible and read about this present.

Write what the present is again here:

Justification

Now think about why this present is awesome? Here's what some students might say:

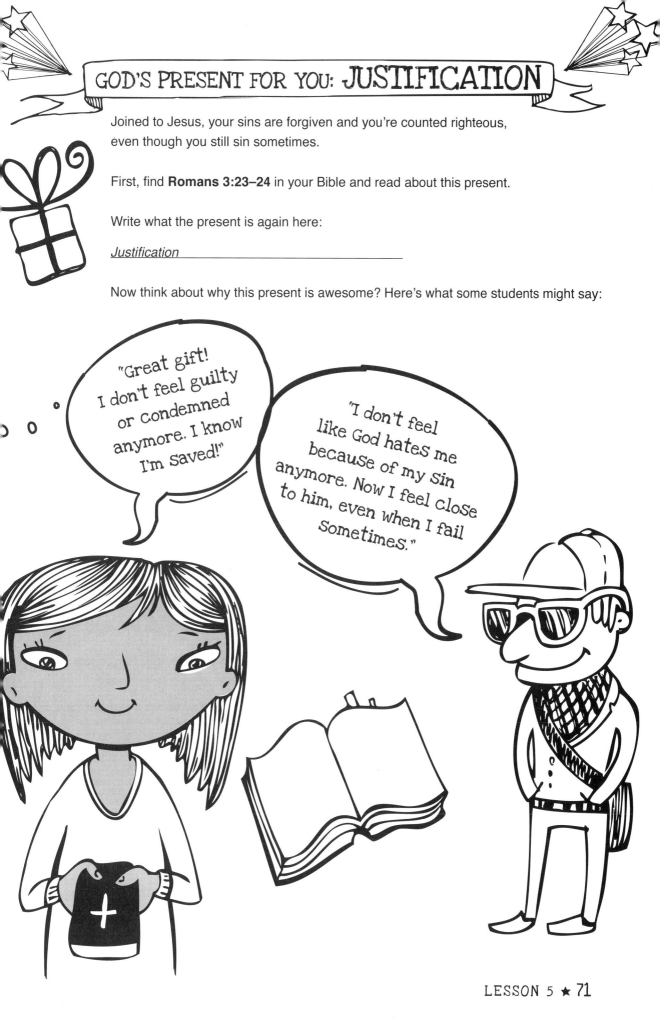

"Great gift! I don't feel guilty or condemned anymore. I know I'm saved!"

"I don't feel like God hates me because of my sin anymore. Now I feel close to him, even when I fail sometimes."

"Wow! Being good doesn't make me feel like showing off anymore. I'm humble because my goodness comes from Jesus."

"Saved only because of Jesus! That means I can stop comparing myself with others or trying to show how much better I am. What a relief!"

Circle the response that feels like the BEST REASON why you personally love this present. Share your answer and explain why you picked it.

Encourage students to think about why they picked the reason they did, and to share it. Doing so will help the group appreciate the value of these gifts from God.

GOD'S PRESENT FOR YOU:
BECOMING GOD'S CHILD

Joined to Jesus, you become God's child, whom he loves, forever. He becomes your Father.

Read about this present in **1 John 3:1**.

Write what the present is again here:

Becoming God's child.

What are some things that make this present wonderful? Read what the students say:

"I can pray to my Father anytime I want and share what's on my heart! He's always glad to listen."

"I can ask my Father for help with any problem anything! I don't need to prove myself first. I know he loves to help me."

"Let's see . . . if I'm God's child, and he only does what's good for me, and he controls everything . . . then everything that happens will work out for my good. Wow!"

"My Father will always keep me near, even after I die. I'll be with him forever. I'm full of hope!"

Put a smiley face next to the response that feels like the BEST REASON why you personally love this present. Share and explain your answer.

GOD'S PRESENT FOR YOU: HOLINESS

Joined to Jesus, you become a new, holy person. Now, with God helping you, you're able to work at becoming more holy and obedient to God all the time.

Romans 6:11 tells about this present. Read it now.

Write what the present is again here:
Holiness

What makes this such an excellent gift? Check out what the students say:

"I'm alive! I can grow as a Christian. I can stop doing disgusting, sinful things. More and more, I'm learning to do good things."

"I have a whole new heart! I'm a changed person. Now I can love what God loves."

"Now the Bible speaks to my heart. I'm working to become like Jesus—imagine that!"

"I can do things that please God! There's no pressure to make him like me, but still I get to enjoy knowing that he's happy with me when I do good things. What a thrill to honor him that way!"

"Even though I still might sin a lot, sin *doesn't* control me anymore. I can fight sin in my life—and WIN!"

Put a big heart-for-God by the response that feels like the BEST REASON why you personally love this present. Share and explain your answer.

TALK ABOUT IT

Sometimes when students are asked what it means to be saved, all they can say is that it means they're going to heaven. But the three presents you just learned about are ways your salvation starts *now*—before you ever get to heaven! List the three presents and think of several *specific examples* of ways your life is changed today when you know you have these presents from God. **Example:** You might tell of something you'll no longer be scared of because you know you're God's child and he always takes good care of you.

You may want to write each present on a whiteboard and list examples students offer. The point of this question is to move beyond the general statements students selected above and talk about specific examples from students' lives at home, school, church, with friends, etc.

★ **Justification:** Specific examples *of being humble, not comparing oneself to others, not trying to impress God*

★ **Becoming God's child:** Specific examples *of desiring to pray, asking for anything, not being afraid, being hopeful*

★ **Holiness:** Specific examples *of loving what God loves, learning to do good, not being controlled by sin*

OPTIONAL STOPPING POINT

If you're stopping the lesson here for today, send your students home with *something to think about* and *prayer*.

SOMETHING TO THINK ABOUT

Tell students: Each of these presents from God goes by several different names. For example, being made God's child is often called "adoption." This week, think about each present and how they help you grow in your faith.

PRAYER

Pray together that you and your students would experience a growing understanding of God's Word, and that a deep joy in the gospel would take root in their hearts this week as they begin to rely more fully on God.

When you restart this lesson later, begin with *review*.

REVIEW

Ask students to tell you the three presents from God from the first half of the lesson that all believers receive. Ask: Did you think of any other ways to describe them in your own words? Use their answers to review the main points about each present.

★ *JUSTIFICATION is God's declaration that you're forgiven and counted righteous in Jesus, even though you still sin sometimes.*

★ *BECOMING GOD'S CHILD (ADOPTION) is having God as your Father who loves, cares for, and disciplines you—and will keep you with himself forever.*

★ *HOLINESS (SANCTIFICATION) means you are a new person who, with God's help, is able and willing to work at always becoming more trusting and obedient.*

PART 2: THE WHOLE ARMOR OF GOD

(40 minutes. Leave plenty of time for prayer at the end of this part of the lesson.)

In this part of the lesson you'll learn how all those presents from God help you fight sin in your life. Using them is like putting on armor from God. The presents make you strong and confident to fight the devil, who tempts you to sin.

The Bible includes a letter Paul wrote to people living in the city of Ephesus.

- ❑ First, Paul reminded them of all God gave them because they were joined to Jesus.

- ❑ Then he told them to live for God. He included things that are hard to do, like telling kids to obey their parents.

- ❑ Then he told them how to fight when the devil tempted them to not obey—by TRUSTING GOD! He called it putting on God's armor: "Be strong in the Lord and in the strength of his might. Put on the whole armor of God, that you may be able to stand against the schemes of the devil" (Ephesians 6:10–11).

 Point to remember: When you fight to not sin, don't try to do it all by yourself. Do it by trusting God.

YOU WOULDN'T WANT TO FIGHT WITHOUT ARMOR, WOULD YOU? SO DON'T TRY TO FIGHT SIN WITHOUT TRUSTING GOD.

Read what Paul wrote in his letter in **Ephesians 6:14–18**. Fill in the blanks below.

*Stand therefore, having fastened on the **belt** of **TRUTH**, and having put on the **breastplate** of **RIGHTEOUSNESS**, and, as **shoes** for your feet, having put on the readiness given by the **GOSPEL OF PEACE**. In all circumstances take up the **shield** of **FAITH**, with which you can extinguish all the flaming darts of the evil one; and take the **helmet** of **SALVATION**, and the **sword** of the Spirit, which is the **WORD OF GOD**, **PRAYING AT ALL TIMES** in the Spirit, with all prayer and supplication.*

Circle the last two items Paul wrote about: the Word of God and praying.

Word of God: God's message for his people. The Bible is the surest Word of God for us—always perfectly true—though God also may speak in other ways, like through preaching that's based on the Bible.

The Word of God and prayer seem different from the other pieces of God's armor, don't they? They're special pieces of armor that a believer should always be using, again and again—every day. Through them, the Holy Spirit gives us power *from God* to fight sin.

We read or listen to the Word of God (again and again, all the time).

We pray (again and again, all the time).

Here are some schemes the devil might use against you, along with ways you might fight back by trusting God and using his armor. How many pieces of armor can you match with each example? Write down each one you notice. (HINT: Each example uses prayer and/or the Word of God, plus at least one more piece of armor. Some may be used more than once.)

| Truth | Righteousness | Gospel of peace Faith |
| Salvation | Word of God | Prayer |

The devil: Tries to convince you that God hasn't done much for you, making you tired of serving God.

You fight back by: Listening to preachers and teachers who tell you the good news of how you have peace with God because Jesus has saved you—and believing that it's true!

And you do it! You serve God.

The armor you used was:

Word of God, gospel of peace, salvation, faith, truth

The devil: Tempts you to lie to your parents.
You fight back by: Praying that God would give you strength to act like the holy, righteous person you are in Jesus.
And you do it! You tell the truth.

The armor you used was:

Prayer, righteousness

The devil: Tells you it's okay to always try to be first in line or to get the best piece of cake or pizza for yourself.
You fight back by: Praying that God would help you think of others first (like Jesus thought of you first when he saved you), then reading in the Bible how God blesses those who are unselfish—and believing that it's true!
And you do it! You let others go first.

The armor you used was:

Prayer, Word of God, truth, salvation

Be sure students understand how in each example they use the Word of God (either read from the Bible or spoken to them) or prayer. The rest of the pieces of armor don't have to be matched exactly to any particular example. Any of them might apply in each example. The point is for students to think about how God's armor is useful in fighting the devil. (Some students might think "faith" is missing from the examples, but it's there. Believing is faith!)

TALK ABOUT IT

Is this the way you usually try to fight sin? Do you trust God and believe in his great presents for you, or do you just try harder by yourself to stop sinning?

SHARING OPPORTUNITY: You as the leader need to be ready to share an example from your own life. Tell of a time when you thought you could resist sin using only your own strength but failed. Or tell how prayer or the Word of God helped you overcome some sin. (NOTE: You and your students should realize that using the armor is not like taking a pill—as if it automatically stopped you from sinning every time. Sometimes you will use the armor and still fail. Other times, as a changed-by-God person, you might resist sin even when you've not been using the armor. But in general, it's wise to constantly use the means God has given us to keep his power working in us.)

Encourage students to share too. As they do, they may have a difficult time distinguishing between effort that is purely self-effort and a relying-on-God sort of effort that still actively involves them in fighting sin. Relying on God does not mean we sit back and do nothing. It means an active life with God—in prayer, in his Word, fostering joy in the gospel—that lives itself out in our battle against sin. We still need to say "no" to sin constantly, but our strength to do that comes from the "armor" we also wear constantly.

LET'S END BY ACTUALLY USING GOD'S ARMOR.

First, use the <u>Word of God</u> and remind yourself of his <u>salvation</u> by reading this Bible passage aloud together.

Praise the LORD, O my soul,
    and forget not all his benefits—

who forgives all your sins
    and heals all your diseases,

who redeems your life from the pit
    and crowns you with love and compassion,

who satisfies your desires with good things
    so that your youth is renewed like the eagle's.

From everlasting to everlasting
    the LORD's love is with those who fear him.

(Psalm 103:2–5, 17 NIV)

Now that you've been reminded how good life with God is, use <u>prayer</u>.

Write a synonym for the word "benefit." _____

<u>Underline</u> God's benefits in the passage from Psalm 103.

Pick two benefits mentioned in the passage you read. Pray as a group, each person thanking God for the gifts they picked.

Pray together that God would keep you thankful and help you resist sin.
Don't be scared to mention specific temptations you have and ask God to give you power over them.

Encourage students to pray for specific temptations they face.

SHARING OPPORTUNITY: You can take the lead here by sharing some of your own temptations. Pick something appropriate to share with your students. Ask them to join you in prayer that you will overcome that temptation.

MAKE IT STICK:
INTERVIEW AN OLDER BELIEVER

(Take 5 minutes at the end of the session to explain the coming week's "Make It Stick" exercise.)

INSTRUCTIONS:

☐ Fill out this Make It Stick page during the week.

☐ Don't forget to bring your *Student Guide* back next time you meet.

☐ If you have time, go ahead and get started now.

Before the next time meeting, conduct a short interview with an older Christian to learn how they grow and obey God better. You can pick a parent or some other adult, but it should be a person who has many years of experience in following Jesus and clearly works to obey him. (HINT: If you can't think of an older believer to interview, ask your leader to be interviewed or to give you suggestions.)

Here are some ideas for questions you might ask that person. You don't have to ask all the questions, just some.

INTERVIEW QUESTIONS:

1. What's the most important thing you do that helps you grow and obey God better?

2. What's a Bible passage that's helped you grow closer to God? Why?

3. How do you pray? What have you learned about how to pray better?

4. What have you given up for Jesus?

Listen carefully to the older Christian and learn from that person. Write down what you find out on the notes page and be ready to report back what you learned the next time you meet.

Some students may struggle to pick a person to interview. You may want to arrange beforehand with a few wise and mature believers to be willing to give interviews, and suggest those people to your students. Parents and other teachers also work well.

What's the most important thing you do that helps you grow and obey God better?

_____

_____

_____

What's a Bible passage that's helped you grow closer to God? Why?

_____

_____

_____

How do you pray? What have you learned about how to pray better?

_____

_____

_____

What have you given up for Jesus?

_____

_____

_____

Other questions you want to ask:

_____

_____

_____

LESSON 6

BUT I'M A GOOD PERSON

Big Idea: Two Kinds of Repentance

NOTES TO THE LEADER

LESSON GOAL

Students will learn that the Christian life involves two kinds of repentance: (1) repentance from sin and (2) repentance from self-justification. They will be urged to believe the good news that their Father loves it when his children repent.

SUMMARY

This lesson begins a unit that takes a deep look at the motives and workings of the heart. The main message of this unit is that working on outward actions alone is NOT the key to being a good Christian; rather, a heart renewed through the gospel of Jesus is necessary for Christian growth.

The lesson is about repentance, which is often thought of as something only bad people have to do.

PART ONE of today's lesson will teach your students how hearts can be enslaved by either sin (BAD behavior) or self-justification (a desire to prove oneself by GOOD behavior). The Christian life means repenting of both.

PART TWO of the lesson will take you and your students through the parable of the prodigal son, which we're treating as a parable about two lost sons. Your students will examine each character in the parable:

★ _The younger son_ is trapped in sin (BAD behavior). He needs to repent of that.

★ _The older son_ is trapped in self-justification (trying to prove himself through GOOD behavior). He needs to repent of that.

★ _The father_ cares for both sons and is eager for each to repent in his own way. The father is a picture of God. Your students will see that God calls them to a life full of repentance—both kinds!—and eagerly welcomes them when they turn away from both sin and self-justification.

In the character of the father, the parable includes one of the Bible's most compelling pictures of the compassion of God and his love for sinners who repent. Part of your job as leader is to make sure your students don't miss this.

NOTE: If you're dividing this lesson into two class sessions, the wrap-up at the optional stopping point contains more material than usual. Look at it in advance and plan your time accordingly.

YOUR PREPARATION

STUDY. The prodigal son parable is the last in a set of three similar parables in Luke 15. Read through the entire chapter and understand the central point these parables make about God's concern for the lost. Also read through the lesson and make sure you understand the premise of teaching about repentance and faith by thinking of it as two kinds of repentance. To repent of sinful behavior and to repent of self-justification—by practicing faith in Jesus—are often paired in the Bible (see Mark 1:15; Luke 24:46–47; Acts 2:38; 20:21; Hebrews 6:1). This lesson makes the point that these two things are how one first becomes a Christian and then also how one continues to grow as a Christian. Be prepared to encourage both unbelieving students and those who are already believers to turn to God by practicing these two things.

BE READY TO SHARE. The lesson invites students to think about the two kinds of repentance by expressing which seems harder for them. In essence, it asks them to consider whether they're more like the younger brother or the older brother in Jesus's parable. You should consider and be prepared to share the same about yourself.

PRAY. Pray that your students will be willing to consider the state of their hearts in this and future lessons, and that God will give them a conviction of sin that makes them able to relate to the brothers in Jesus's parable. Pray also that they will see the Father's compassion for people who repent and will be eager to make repentance central to their lives.

BEFORE YOU BEGIN

(10 minutes)

Report on your interview with the older believer. What did you learn about the Christian life? Did anything surprise you?

Did the older believer tell you something about **fighting sin**? If so, share it with the group.

Did the older believer tell you something about **trusting Jesus**? If so, share it with the group.

Encourage students to share what they learned from their interviews. Today's lesson is about repentance (fighting sin) and faith (trusting Jesus), so pay particular attention to how both of these activities mark the Christian life.

TODAY'S LESSON

Think about how you breathe. You INHALE and you EXHALE. They go together. You can't do one without the other. You can't live unless you do *both*.

The Christian life is like breathing. You fight sin (we call that REPENTANCE) and you trust Jesus (we call that FAITH). They always go together. You need *both* in order to live and grow as a Christian. That's what you'll learn about today.

PART 1: TWO KINDS OF REPENTANCE

(20 minutes)

In this section, you'll learn how you can also think of REPENTANCE and FAITH as two difference kinds of repentance.

Jesus talked about both when he first started preaching. Read what he said:

> *"The kingdom of God is at hand; repent and believe in the gospel." (Mark 1:15)*

Underline the two things Jesus said to do.

Belief in the gospel means the same thing as faith. Let's define the two things Jesus said to do.

Repent: Stop living a wrong way and start living a new, godly way.

Have faith: Believe that Jesus died for your sin and trust him—not your own good behavior to make you right with God.

Point to remember:
To become a Christian, *start* practicing repentance and faith in Jesus.
To grow as a Christian, *keep* practicing repentance and faith in Jesus.

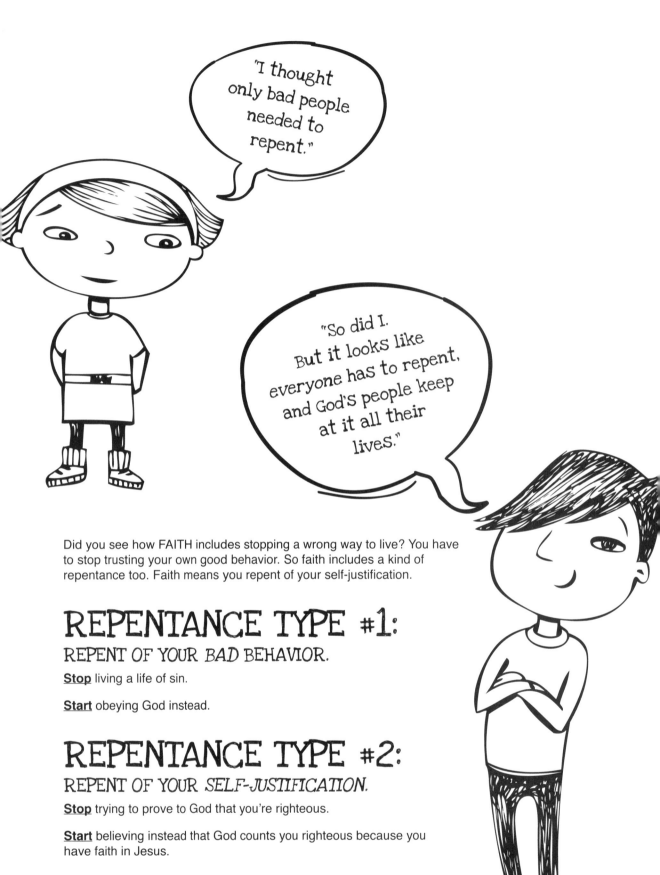

"I thought only bad people needed to repent."

"So did I. But it looks like everyone has to repent, and God's people keep at it all their lives."

Did you see how FAITH includes stopping a wrong way to live? You have to stop trusting your own good behavior. So faith includes a kind of repentance too. Faith means you repent of your self-justification.

REPENTANCE TYPE #1:
REPENT OF YOUR *BAD* BEHAVIOR.

Stop living a life of sin.

Start obeying God instead.

REPENTANCE TYPE #2:
REPENT OF YOUR *SELF-JUSTIFICATION*.

Stop trying to prove to God that you're righteous.

Start believing instead that God counts you righteous because you have faith in Jesus.

Draw a circle around the type of repentance that seems harder to you. Are you mostly . . .

A SINNER

You try to make yourself happy by being BAD and living however you want.

You especially need to repent of your BAD BEHAVIOR.

OR

A SELF-JUSTIFIER

You try to earn a happy life by being GOOD and living how you're supposed to (and you compare yourself to others and get jealous).

You especially need to repent of your SELF-JUSTIFICATION.

TALK ABOUT IT

Tell why that kind of repentance is harder for you.

Encourage students to talk about their approach to life and to God.

- ★ *Are they resisting God's law and living as they like?*
- ★ *Or are they trying to impress God by being good (and getting either proud or insecure about their performance)?*

It's surely some of both, but picking a main tendency will help them think about the matter.

TIP: If you have time, or if you need help getting your students to discuss this, you might want to refer back to the students with "blurry gospel vision" in lesson one. The SMUG and NERVOUS students especially need to repent of self-justification. The ALL-ABOUT-ME and EASY LIFE students especially need to repent of sin.

PART 2: THE TWO SONS

(Allow 55 minutes if done in one class session. If the lesson is presented in two sessions, allow 20 minutes during the first session to introduce and discuss the parable of the two sons. The second part consists of 45 minutes covering the character sketches and application.)

For the rest of this lesson, you'll study a story Jesus told about two sons. Each son especially needed one type of repentance.

First read about the crowd that heard Jesus's story. They needed to repent too.

> *Now the tax collectors and sinners were all drawing near to hear him. And the Pharisees and the scribes grumbled, saying, "This man receives sinners and eats with them." (Luke 15:1–2)*

Jesus told his story to two kinds of people. Which groups do you think were people who did BAD things and needed to repent of their <u>bad behavior</u>?

<u>Tax collectors</u>_____ and <u>sinners</u>_____

Which groups do you think were people who did GOOD things, but compared themselves to others and needed to repent of their <u>self-justification</u>?

<u>Pharisees</u>_____ and <u>scribes</u>_____

Tax collectors in those days cheated people to get rich (obviously BAD!). Pharisees were a group of people who worked hard to obey God (obviously GOOD!). But Jesus wanted both kinds of people to see that they need him.

OPTIONAL STOPPING POINT

If you're dividing this lesson into two class sessions, take a break here.

If you're dividing this lesson into two class sessions, end today's class by discussing with your students how you and they are similar to the younger or older son in Jesus's parable:

Read the entire parable from Luke 15:11–32.

Ask: Which of the sons was bad and which was trying to prove how good he was? Which are you most like?

Have students give examples of how their behavior is often similar to that of one of the sons. Ask them: How does this mean you need to repent?

It may help to mark responses on a whiteboard, keeping a tally of how many students think they're "bad sons" and how many see themselves as "good sons." In most classes made up of students who are familiar with church and the Bible, it's especially important that "good son" students come to see their need to repent of self-justification.

Now send your students home with *something to think about* and *prayer*.

SOMETHING TO THINK ABOUT

Tell students: This week keep thinking about which son in Jesus's story you are most like and how you need to repent.

PRAYER

Pray together that your students' hearts would be renewed and captured by the gospel. Pray for each student that they would draw closer to God and repent of both sin and self-righteousness.

When you restart this lesson later, begin with *review*.

REVIEW

Ask students: What are the two ways to repent that we studied in the first part of this lesson? (Repenting of BAD BEHAVIOR and repenting of SELF-JUSTIFICATION.) Review what they mean if necessary. Remind the students of Jesus's parable of the two sons, which you'll begin reading again to start the second half of the lesson.

Did you notice how the younger son asked for his inheritance while the father was still alive? That's like saying you wish your father were dead already! Then he went out and wasted it.

Character Sketch:
Younger Son

Now do a character sketch of the younger son in this first part of the story. Think of at least four adjectives that describe his character. Write them next to his picture. If you need help thinking of words to describe him, consider these questions:

❑   What is his attitude?

❑   How does he feel about others?

❑   How well does he contribute to his family?

❑   What is it about him that gets him into trouble?

Also consider what the younger son thinks will make him happy in life. Write a sentence in the thought bubble that describes what he's hoping for at the start of the story.

Share and discuss the words and sentences you thought of.

Encourage students to keep thinking about the son until they come up with several words to describe him. Possible answers include: Selfish, disrespectful, uncaring, unhelpful, rebellious, greedy, wasteful, foolish, hurtful, wild, sinful. Help students to see that he thinks a life where he can do whatever he wants will make him happy.

Finally, circle the description that best fits the younger son.

A SINNER

You try to make yourself happy by being BAD and living however you want.

You especially need to repent of your BAD BEHAVIOR.

A SELF-JUSTIFIER

You try to earn a happy life by being GOOD and living how you're supposed to (and you compare yourself to others and get jealous).

You especially need to repent of your SELF-JUSTIFICATION.

Now read what happened with the younger son in verses 17–24.

The younger son repented! He went home and found the father to be more loving than he ever imagined. Only a father—the best father you could imagine—could have *that* much love. It was humiliating for an older man in Jesus's day to run. But the father was so happy to see his son that he ran to greet him!

List six other things the father did because he was so happy to see his son.

1. _____

2. _____

3. _____

4. _____

5. _____

6. _____

The father in the story is like God. What do you think Jesus wanted the sinners who were listening to his story to know about God? Write your answer in a sentence below or discuss with the group.

_____

_____

_____

Help students to see that the point of the story is that God is eager to welcome sinners who repent. He has much compassion on them. He is overjoyed when one turns back to him.
(It's okay to deal with this question quickly, as we'll come back to this theme later in the lesson.)

The story isn't over. Read verses 25–32 to learn what the older son did when he heard about the celebration.

Character Sketch: Older Son

Now do a character sketch of the older son. Again think of adjectives that describe him, and write them next to his picture. If you need help, consider these questions:

❏ How well does he contribute to his family and work for his father?

❏ How might he compare himself to his younger brother?

❏ How does he feel about the party?

❏ What is his attitude toward his father?

Then imagine what the older son thinks is the way to be happy and get good things in life. Write a sentence in the thought bubble that describes his plan to get approval from the father and feel good about himself.

Share and discuss the words and sentences you thought of.

> *Possible answers include: Obedient, hard-working, deserving, good, resentful, angry, jealous, bitter. The older son is trying to earn his father's approval and feel good about himself by being a good, obedient son. He thinks he deserves good things because he's been a good son.*

Now circle the description that best fits the older son.

A SINNER

You try to make yourself happy by being BAD and living however you want.

You especially need to repent of your BAD BEHAVIOR.

OR

A SELF-JUSTIFIER

You try to earn a happy life by being GOOD and living how you're supposed to (and you compare yourself to others and get jealous).

You especially need to repent of your SELF-JUSTIFICATION.

Character sketch: Father

There's one more character sketch to do. It's for the most important character in the story—the father. Refer back to the story in your Bible if necessary. Write some adjectives that describe him next to his picture.

Also fill in two thought bubbles for the father:

❑ **First thought bubble:** Imagine what the father is thinking now that his younger son has repented of his sin.

❑ **Second thought bubble:** Imagine what the father hopes for his older son.

Share and discuss what you wrote.

Possible answers include: Loving, compassionate, forgiving, celebrating, overjoyed, caring, understanding. Students might relate to the older son and have some negative feelings about the father as well—words like "unfair." If so, help them to see that the father's character is not unfair. He's just so eager to celebrate repentant sinners that his compassion may seem unfair at first glance.

The father's feeling toward the younger son is joy and compassion in the son's repentance of sin. His hope for his older son is that the son will repent of his jealousy and his trying-to-please, self-justifying attitude.

TALK ABOUT IT

Jesus's story about the two sons matters when YOU need to repent.

SITUATION #1: You've <u>behaved</u> badly by living your way instead of God's way.

What should you remember about your Father in heaven? How does he feel about his children who've behaved badly?

*Help students to see that their Father in heaven still loves them. He's eager for them to repent and to welcome them back—no matter how bad they've been. He loves them because Jesus died for them. There's nothing they can do that's so **bad** it'll make God love them **less**.*

SITUATION #2: You're trying <u>self-justification</u>, hoping to earn God's love by being good.

Now what should you remember about your Father in heaven? How does he feel about his children who've tried to justify themselves?

*Help students to see that their Father in heaven wants them to understand what the older son needed to understand—that everything he has is theirs, for free! He loves them too because Jesus died for them. There's nothing they can do that's so **good** it'll make God love them **more**.*

The father in Jesus's story told the older son, "Everything I have is yours." Wow! Here's a list of some of the things you already have from God and don't need to earn if you have faith in Jesus.

- ❏ God loves you perfectly, forever. (Psalm 136:1)
- ❏ God adopts you as his own son/daughter. (John 1:12)
- ❏ God promises to never leave you for any reason. (Hebrews 13:5)
- ❏ God makes everything work for your good. (Romans 8:28)
- ❏ God gives you an inheritance in heaven that you can't lose. (1 Peter 1:4)
- ❏ God will give you eternal joy with him. (Revelation 7:17)

PRAY ABOUT IT

Make your closing prayer today a prayer of thanksgiving for the items on that list. Thank God for many of them, checking them off as you mention them to him. Then pray that he will help you believe that he's *that* good and loving. Pray that this will help you repent of both your <u>bad behavior</u> and your <u>self-justification</u>.

Much of this lesson has been about ways your students, like the sons in the parable, might fail. For that reason, it's important to make sure this ending prayer time stays thankful and focused on the gospel blessings that come from our Father. Don't let your students leave discouraged. Instead, help them to be encouraged by how their Father has a solution for both sin and self-justification, and how he has compassion on those who repent of both.

MAKE IT STICK:

SPEND TIME WITH YOUR FATHER

(Take 5 minutes at the end of the session to explain the coming week's "Make It Stick" exercise.)

INSTRUCTIONS:

❑ Fill out this Make It Stick page during the week.

❑ Don't forget to bring your *Student Guide* back next time you meet.

Jesus's story about the two sons was actually the last in a series of three similar parables. In each one, something is lost and the person who lost it has a great celebration when it's found.

Your task until the next session is to spend time with your Father in prayer *every day*, thanking him for the love and compassion he had for you when you were still lost in sin. He celebrates how you're saved! So this week, celebrate with him.

Do three things in each day's time with God (yes, the same thing each day):

1. Read the first two stories in Luke 15:1–10.

2. Remember how lost you were before God saved you. You were *dead* in sin.

3. Thank God in your own words for the amazing love he has for someone like you: "But God, being rich in mercy, because of the great love with which he loved us, even when we were dead in our trespasses, made us alive together with Christ—by grace you have been saved" (Ephesians 2:4–5).

Each day, after you pray, write down one thing you thanked God for in your prayer.

Day One:
Thank you, Father, that you _____ me.

Day Two:
Thank you, Father, that you _____ me.

Day Three:
Thank you, Father, that you _____ me.

Day Four:
Thank you, Father, that you _____ me.

Day Five:
Thank you, Father, that you _____ me.

Day Six
Thank you, Father, that you _____ me.

Day Seven:
Thank you, Father, that you _____ me.

DO I LOVE GOD? UM...

Big Idea: Big Forgiveness and Big Love

NOTES TO THE LEADER

LESSON GOAL

Students will learn to admit that they are BIG sinners, but also believe that they have BIG forgiveness in Jesus—giving them BIG love for their Savior.

SUMMARY

This lesson builds a case for your students to admit their sin. It teaches this as a necessary first step in growing in love for God. The case is built in three parts:

PART ONE teaches that we have two choices when we sin: we can ignore and hide our sin, or we can admit it. Only admitting our sin allows us to experience forgiveness in Jesus and love for him—but admitting sin is scary and embarrassing! Your students will be encouraged to talk about why they hesitate to admit their sin.

PART TWO studies the account of Jesus's attendance at a dinner hosted by Simon the Pharisee, and of the sinful woman who came and washed his feet. Your students will see how Simon, despite looking like a "better" person, had little love for Jesus because he had little sense of his forgiveness—while the woman who admitted her sin loved much because she'd been forgiven much.

PART THREE lets you and your students fill in a figure that shows how a growing appreciation of forgiveness is needed if one is to grow in love for Christ. Your students will see how admitting their sin, and then believing in a bigger cross, leads to bigger Christian growth.

YOUR PREPARATION

STUDY. This lesson contains more reading than most, so be prepared for extended reading broken up by short opportunities for discussion. Read through the lesson beforehand and make sure you understand its arguments so that you can answer questions when they come up. The figure with the growing cross can be tricky for young people to follow, so make sure you look at it carefully and can explain it properly. Its main point is that Christian growth stalls unless we're constantly growing in our appreciation for how much we're forgiven in Jesus.

BE READY TO SHARE. Since admitting sin is a big theme of this lesson, it's important that you as the leader prepare to take the lead in confession. There are two places in particular where you should be ready with specific examples of how you fail:

★ At the end of the study of Simon and the sinful woman, be ready with an example of how you've failed to act like the woman and been more like Simon instead.

★ At the end of the lesson, be ready to talk about specific ways you've sometimes tried to hide your sin and how your Christian life would be better if you didn't do that.

PRAY. Pray that your students would experience the sweetness of confession of sin and forgiveness. You might want to pray for each student that his or her life would be like the final picture in the cross figure.

BEFORE YOU BEGIN

(10 minutes)

Tell about the time you spent with your Father reading Luke 15 and praying.
Tell what things you liked about it or what you didn't like about it.

Did you get **bored**? _____ Yes _____ No

If you're bored with God, it might mean you trust other things besides Jesus to really
make you happy.

<u>So next time you pray</u>: Repent of your sin (how you love other things more than Jesus).
Confess your sin to your Father and ask him to help you see the beauty of Jesus.

Did it make you **uncomfortable**? _____ Yes _____ No

If you aren't comfortable with God, it might mean you feel your behavior isn't good enough
for him. Remember that you may always pray to God—not because you're good enough, but
because you're joined to Jesus and have his righteousness.

<u>So next time you pray</u>: Repent of your self-justification. Your Father loves for you to come to him
no matter how bad you've been.

*Encourage students to be honest about both their joys and their struggles in prayer. It's easy
for believers to feel condemned when they think about their prayer lives, so be sure to remind
strugglers of the gospel. Part of the good news of Jesus is that God has made prayer something
that never needs to feel condemning no matter how bad we are at it! This is because:*

1. *We only pray in the first place because we're joined to Jesus and he is good. Prayer never
   depends on us being good. "Since then we have a great high priest who has passed through
   the heavens, Jesus, the Son of God, let us hold fast our confession. For we do not have a
   high priest who is unable to sympathize with our weaknesses, but one who in every respect
   has been tempted as we are, yet without sin. Let us then with confidence draw near to the
   throne of grace, that we may receive mercy and find grace to help in time of need" (Hebrews
   4:14–16).*

2. *Prayer is between the Father and his child. God is eager to hear our prayers because we're
   his children. "When you pray, say: Father" (Luke 11:2).*

3. *The Holy Spirit is there to help us, not scold us. He knows we're weak and wants to help us.
   "The Spirit helps us in our weakness. For we do not know what to pray for as we ought,
   but the Spirit himself intercedes for us with groanings too deep for words" (Romans 8:26).*

If necessary, be ready to encourage your students with these verses.

TODAY'S LESSON

Wouldn't it be nice to love God so much that you're always eager to spend time with your Father? Today you'll learn how your love for Jesus can grow—when you admit you're a sinner!

PART 1: TWO CHOICES WHEN YOU SIN

(15 minutes)

Let's start by learning about two choices you have when you realize you've sinned. Read this story:

When I was a new Christian, I began to read my Bible as often as I could. One day as I was reading how God hated sin, and how our sin separates us from him, I thought, *Since God hates sin so much, today I won't sin the entire day. I am going to have a sin-free day!*

As soon as I finished thinking I could have a "sin-free" day, I saw my brother riding my bike without my permission. The next instant I was outside and yelling at him to get off my bike. How dare he touch my stuff!

Then it hit me. Oh, no! I was being selfish. I couldn't keep sin out of my life for even five seconds, let alone a whole day. For the first time, I saw how big my sin was!

Yikes! I was in big trouble!

Maybe you've had an experience like that. You realized how terribly hard it is to not sin for even a short while. When you realize what a big sinner you are, you have **two choices**.

CHOICE #1:

You can <u>try to ignore your sin or hide it</u>, like these students.

"I won't think about my sin because I don't want to feel bad."

"I just can't admit something embarrassing."

"I'll just pretend God doesn't care so much."

"Maybe it'll fix itself someday."

"As long as nobody notices my sin, others will still think well of me."

"Maybe I can convince God I'm okay if I still go to church and pray and stuff."

Why will it be hard for those students to grow as Christians when they're thinking these ways? Discuss.

Don't worry about right answers at this point. Just let students briefly discuss the question to start thinking about it. The explanation of why the students won't grow is coming on the next page.

CHOICE #2:

The other choice is to <u>admit you're a horrible sinner</u>. That's what we'll do in the next several lessons. To complete these lessons, you're going to have to think and talk LOTS about your own sin and the ways you do wrong. It'll be SIN, SIN, SIN.

How does that sound to you? Check all the lines that apply.

____ It sounds like **no fun**. I might end up feeling bad about myself. I wish we could pretend God doesn't care so much about sin.

____ It sounds like it might be **embarrassing**. I need to think of some not-so-bad sins I can tell about—so I can avoid telling about my very worst ones.

____ It sounds **scary**. I don't like thinking about myself that way, or what might happen to me because of my sin.

TALK ABOUT IT

Show the group which lines you checked. If none of them are what you feel when you have to talk about your sin, tell what you do feel.

Encourage students to be honest about how admitting their sin and talking about it makes them feel. It's common for this to be uncomfortable.

The idea that our sin makes us feel embarrassed may deserve special attention. There's a sense in which shame over sin is a good thing. It means the Spirit is at work, affecting the conscience. But a deep embarrassment that makes us want to hide is a sign that we aren't fully appreciating the forgiveness and status that is ours in Christ. As saved people we can freely admit our sin and, even though we know that what we've done is shameful, stand as unashamed people before God and each other. Jesus has removed our shame.

Whenever you try to ignore or hide your sin, it's <u>hard for you to grow</u>.

❑ Because you're **scared** or **unhappy** when you hear how God feels about sin, you won't enjoy studying about him or reading the Bible. You'll stop learning about God.

❑ Because you're too **scared** or **embarrassed** to admit your sin, you'll keep hiding it. Instead of learning new ways to repent, you'll pretend you don't have to repent.

PART 2: SIMON AND THE SINFUL WOMAN

(20 minutes)

Now let's study a Bible story from **Luke 7:36–47**. First learn about the characters and the occasion.

Simon
(a Pharisee)

Respected in the city

Well-known as a person who worked hard to obey God

Everyone thought, "Good for you!"

Sinful Woman

Had a bad reputation in the city

Well-known as a person who did sinful things

Everyone thought, "Shame on you!"

OCCASION:

A meal, hosted by Simon, which Jesus attended

Anyone in the city could watch and listen, but only invited guests could sit and eat

Very honored guests were greeted by Simon with a kiss

Guests with master status had their feet washed by a servant

THE STORY BEGINS:
A dinner surprise.

Read through verse 39 and answer the questions below.

Which character focuses on the sins of others instead of his/her own sins?

Simon

Which character thinks him/herself so good he/she can judge others?

Simon

Is this "good" person the same character who most shows love to Jesus?

_No_

THE STORY CONTINUES: Jesus explains

Read vv. 40–47.

Jesus said having sins forgiven is like owing money and having the debt canceled so you don't have to pay.

Circle the one that makes you most thankful.

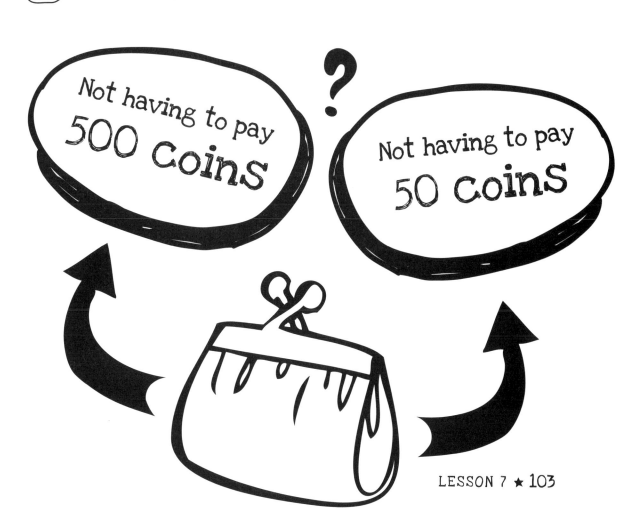

Circle the character who loved Jesus most.

Woman who was forgiven for MUCH sin

Simon who was forgiven little

Do you think Simon really didn't sin much? Or do you think his sin was just less obvious or better hidden? Discuss why you think so.

Though we can't know for sure how big a sinner Simon was, we know that everyone sins greatly. It's a safe bet to suggest he didn't realize the full extent of his sin, even if, as a Pharisee, he searched his heart for sin daily. The story itself reveals that Simon took a superior and condescending attitude toward others, including Jesus—so he was guilty of that sin, at least.

For each statement, write whether you suspect it better fits Simon or the woman.

The woman   Was so sorry for sin it made him/her cry.

The woman   Knew his/her life had been shameful.

Simon   Thought his/her life was a model for others.

Simon   Had little joy over being forgiven and seldom thought about it much.

Simon   Was uninterested in loving Jesus.

The woman   Was eager to show love for Jesus.

TALK ABOUT IT

Now look back over the list. Which statements best describe <u>you</u>? Share how you're like Simon or like the sinful woman.

If students are honest, it's likely some of them will see a lot of themselves in Simon. Help them to see the connection between having joy (or not) over being forgiven and having much love (or not) for Jesus.

SHARING OPPORTUNITY: To show that it's safe to admit sin, it may be important here for you to admit how you sometimes act or think like Simon or fail to act like the woman. Try to give a specific example of a time it happened. You can also share examples of success and growth, of course.

The woman knew how big and shameful her sin was. Remember, everyone thought "shame on you!" about her.

When Jesus forgives your sin, he takes away your guilt and shame. When he died on the cross, people passing by thought he was a criminal. They thought "shame on you!"—about HIM! That's what <u>you</u> deserve, but Jesus took it in your place.

The MORE you understand how shameful your sin is and how he took <u>all</u> of that **guilt** and **punishment** and **shame** for you on the cross, the MORE you will love him! *That's* how you grow.

OPTIONAL STOPPING POINT

If you're dividing this lesson into two class sessions, take a break here.

If you're stopping the lesson here for today, send your students home with *something to think about* and *prayer*.

SOMETHING TO THINK ABOUT

Tell students: Remember that if you believe in Jesus you are a dearly loved child of God. Absolutely nothing can separate you from his love (Romans 8:38–39). This week, think about why it helps to know you're loved that much even though you've sinned lots. How can that help you to live more like the sinful woman and less like Simon?

PRAYER

Pray together that your students would experience a growing awareness of their own sinfulness and, even more, a growing awareness of how much they are forgiven in Jesus. Pray for each student that he or she would continue to grow in faith and in love for Jesus.

When you restart this lesson later, begin with *review*.

REVIEW

Remind students of the story of Jesus, Simon, and the sinful woman. Let them tell you about each of the characters and what happened. Be sure to cover the following points:

★ *The woman knew how big and shameful her sin was. Everyone thought "shame on you!" about her.*

★ *When Jesus forgives your sin, he takes away your guilt and shame. When he died on the cross, people passing by thought he was a criminal. They thought: "Shame on you!" — about HIM! That's what you deserve, but Jesus took it in your place.*

★ *The MORE you understand how shameful your sin is and how he took all of that guilt and punishment and shame for you on the cross, the MORE you will love him! That's how you grow.*

PART 3: THE CROSS FIGURE

(About 45 minutes)

The four parts of the cross figure will help you understand how important it is to admit that your sin is BIG and to believe that your forgiveness in Jesus is BIG too.

Cross figure part 1 shows your life when you're a new Christian. The light stands for two things you see when you believe. First, you see how holy God is and how he wants you to be holy too (the top of the beam of light). Second, you see how sinful and unholy you actually are (the bottom of the beam of light).

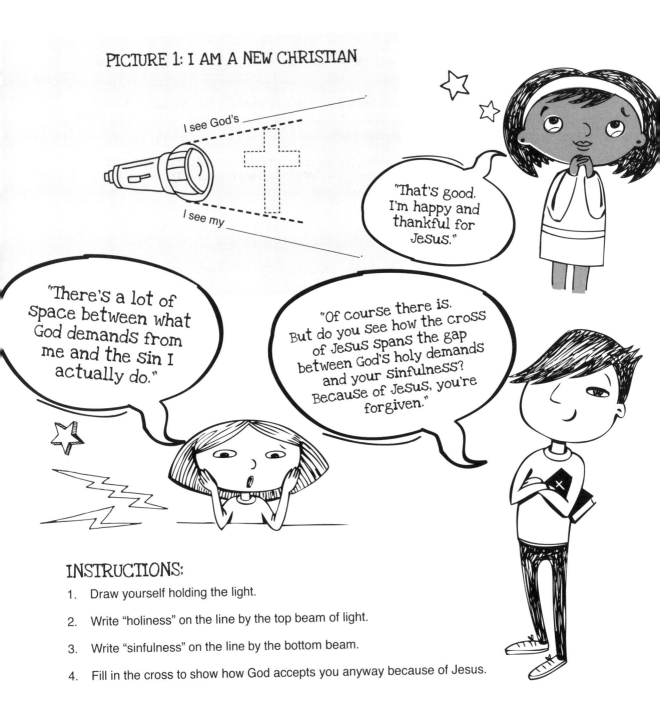

PICTURE 1: I AM A NEW CHRISTIAN

I see God's _____

I see my _____

"That's good. I'm happy and thankful for Jesus."

"There's a lot of space between what God demands from me and the sin I actually do."

"Of course there is. But do you see how the cross of Jesus spans the gap between God's holy demands and your sinfulness? Because of Jesus, you're forgiven."

INSTRUCTIONS:

1. Draw yourself holding the light.

2. Write "holiness" on the line by the top beam of light.

3. Write "sinfulness" on the line by the bottom beam.

4. Fill in the cross to show how God accepts you anyway because of Jesus.

The second part of the cross figure shows that you've learned MORE about God's holy demands. You've also learned MORE about how sinful you are. The beam of light is growing wider.

PICTURE 2: I LEARN MORE

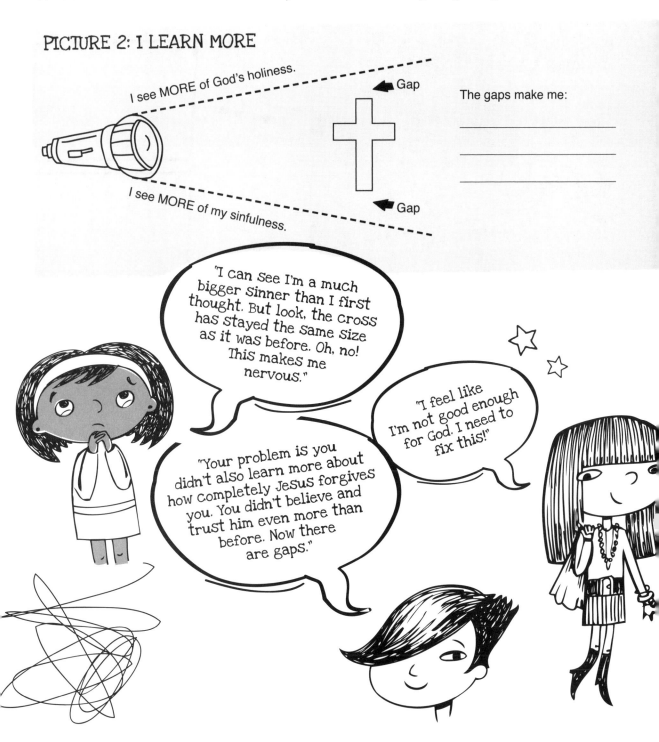

I see MORE of God's holiness.

← Gap

← Gap

I see MORE of my sinfulness.

The gaps make me:

_____

_____

_____

"I can see I'm a much bigger sinner than I first thought. But look, the cross has stayed the same size as it was before. Oh, no! This makes me nervous."

"I feel like I'm not good enough for God. I need to fix this!"

"Your problem is you didn't also learn more about how completely Jesus forgives you. You didn't believe and trust him even more than before. Now there are gaps."

INSTRUCTIONS:

1. Fill in the too-small cross that won't let you feel completely accepted by God.

2. Write the words "scared," "unhappy," and "embarrassed" on the blank lines.

In the third part of the cross figure, you start pretending. Because you're worried and embarrassed at not being good enough, you try to fill in the gaps yourself. You pretend God really doesn't care so much about some sins. Or you make excuses for your sin so you'll look like a better person than you really are.

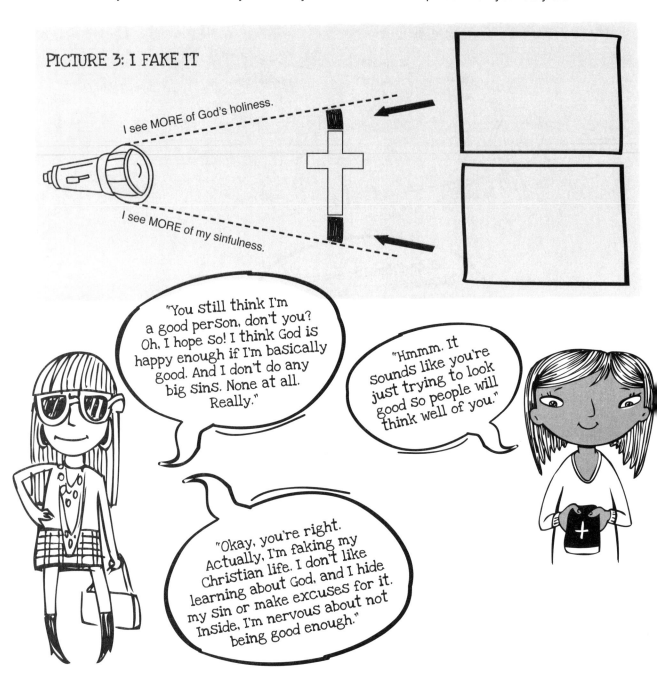

PICTURE 3: I FAKE IT

I see MORE of God's holiness.

I see MORE of my sinfulness.

"You still think I'm a good person, don't you? Oh, I hope so! I think God is happy enough if I'm basically good. And I don't do any big sins. None at all. Really."

"Hmmm. It sounds like you're just trying to look good so people will think well of you."

"Okay, you're right. Actually, I'm faking my Christian life. I don't like learning about God, and I hide my sin or make excuses for it. Inside, I'm nervous about not being good enough."

INSTRUCTIONS:

1. In the top box write, "I pretend God doesn't mind my sin."

2. In the bottom box write, "I pretend I'm better than I really am."

In part 4 of the cross figure, you stop pretending and start trusting Jesus MORE instead. You admit your sin is huge, but you believe that God still forgives all of it because Jesus died for you. The cross and all that Jesus does for you seems *that big* to you because you're trusting him *that much!*

PICTURE 4: I CAN REALLY GROW

I see MORE of God's holiness.

I see MORE of my sinfulness.

What Jesus does for me seems bigger too! I believe MORE that I am:

_____
_____
_____
_____

because of Jesus.

"I've learned that my sin is so big I have no chance of covering it up with excuses. But good news! God loves me SO much that he still forgives me for all that yucky sin."

"It feels good to have bigger belief, doesn't it?"

"Yes. Now that I believe in Jesus MORE, all that he does for me seems bigger. Instead of trusting my excuses to make me look good, I trust Jesus to forgive everything. Now I can learn about God and admit my sin and enjoy it! I can grow! I love Jesus more too."

INSTRUCTIONS:

1. Fill in the larger cross that covers all your sin.

2. On the lines write:

- "forgiven"
- "loved"
- "accepted"
- "righteous"
- "unashamed"

Part 4 of the cross figure teaches that whenever you sin you have **two choices.**

Choice 1 → **When I Sin** → Get scared. Make excuses. Try to make myself look better than I am. → No growth. No love for Jesus.

Choice 2 → **When I Sin** → Admit it. Trust Jesus. Believe that he died for all my sin. His love for me is that big! → Growth. Bigger love for Jesus.

Which choice treats Jesus's death as a little thing you don't need very much?
Which treats it as a big thing that means the world to you?

The second choice treats Jesus's death as a big thing in one's life. Help students to see that Christian growth and love for Jesus are connected to admitting sin and a big belief in the cross and forgiveness.

TALK ABOUT IT

How would your behavior change if you made the second choice more often?

Urge students to think of concrete, practical ways they would behave differently if they more fully trusted in the cross instead of in making excuses and trying to look good. On a whiteboard, you might want to list settings students find themselves in (at school, with friends, with parents, with brothers and sisters, playing sports, playing a game, dividing snacks, etc.) and ask them about their behavior in those situations. Remember to focus on how they might act when caught sinning. Will they hide it or admit it and repent? It would be appropriate to pray after this discussion as well, thanking God for the bigness of salvation and asking him for help to more fully believe it and love him for it.

SHARING OPPORTUNITY: Be prepared to share an example from your own life of a time when you tried to hide or ignore your sin. Tell how your behavior would have been different if you'd admitted your sin and trusted the cross instead—or how you're growing more as a Christian now that you do.

MAKE IT STICK:

ADMIT YOUR SIN

(Take 5 minutes at the end of the session to explain the coming week's "Make It Stick" exercise.)

INSTRUCTIONS:

❑   Fill out this Make It Stick page during the week.

❑   Don't forget to bring your *Student Guide* back next time you meet.

❑   If you have time, go ahead and get started now.

Memorize 1 John 1:8–9.

> *If we say we have no sin, we deceive ourselves, and the truth is not in us. If we confess our sins, he is faithful and just to forgive us our sins and to cleanse us from all unrighteousness.*

Fill your name in the first part of the verse:

If I, _____, say that I have no sin, I, _____, deceive myself and the truth is not in me.

This week, notice when you: try to defend yourself or make excuses for your sin, instead of stopping, admitting you were wrong, and asking forgiveness.

Below, write a few sentences about . . .

. . . a time this week when you caught yourself making excuses for your sin, and how the situation could have been different if you'd admitted your sin and asked forgiveness instead, or

. . . a time this week when you remembered to admit your sin instead of hiding it, and how it felt to do this.

_____

_____

_____

_____

_____

_____

_____

_____

_____

YES, I WORSHIP IDOLS

Big Idea: Real-Life Idols

NOTES TO THE LEADER

This lesson has no optional stopping point and should not be divided. If you have a short class period and normally divide lessons into two sessions, you may need to work through this lesson a bit more quickly than usual to get through it in time. If you have a long class period, use the optional discussion questions in part 1 of this lesson to spend more time discussing idols and worship with your students.

LESSON GOAL

Students will identify the idols in their lives, see how Jesus is better, and begin repenting of their idol worship.

SUMMARY

The previous lesson taught the importance of admitting sin. This one, along with the next, examines the underlying reasons why we sin. Everyone has idols that lead to sinful behavior.

PART ONE will introduce your students to the reasons for idol worship, using idol worshipers in the Bible (in Phoenicia and Greece) as examples. People tend to worship idols for at least one of three reasons:

1. *The idol promises something they <u>love</u> more than they love God.*

2. *The idol is something they <u>trust</u> more than they trust God.*

3. *The idol is something they <u>fear</u> losing more than they fear God.*

PART TWO deals with modern-day idols common among many students (popularity, success, approval, money, comforts, and more). Your students will have to think about what they love, trust, and fear in life—and identify their personal idols.

PART THREE shows how Jesus is better than any idol, using examples from the Bible of how Paul and Elijah spoke to idol worshipers in Greece and Phoenicia. The lesson ends with prayer, thanking God for being better than our idols and asking him to help us repent of them.

YOUR PREPARATION

STUDY. In addition to reading through the lesson, read the two Bible accounts it's built on:

★ *Elijah's contest with the priests of Baal in 1 Kings 20–46*

★ *Paul's speech in Athens in Acts 17:16–34*

If it sounds strange to you that nonphysical desires and fears can be idols, contemplate Colossians 3:5; "Put to death therefore what is earthly in you: sexual immorality, impurity, passion, evil desire, and covetousness, which is idolatry." We covet so many things, and the Bible teaches that anything coming before God in our lives is an idol.

BE READY TO SHARE. In the second part of the lesson, you will have an opportunity to share what sorts of things you get tempted to put before God. Look through the list ahead of time and be ready to share an idol that tempts you and the sort of sinful behavior it can lure you into. Also be ready to share how Jesus is actually better than that idol—and how he helps you to repent.

PRAY. Pray that both you and your students would experience the godly conviction of sin that leads to repentance. Pray also for opportunities throughout the lesson to show them the beauty of Jesus; that they would see how much more glorious he is than any idol.

BEFORE YOU BEGIN

(10 minutes, if you have a long class session. If your time is limited to an hour or less, skip this discussion and just start with Today's Lesson)

Share what you wrote about a time when you caught yourself making excuses for your sin. Did you remember to admit your sin and seek forgiveness instead?

Why do you think that's often hard to do?

It's often the case that we don't like admitting sin and asking forgiveness again and again because it hurts our pride or makes us feel dishonest. Remind students that big love for Jesus starts with admitting our sin instead of hiding it and knowing the largeness of our forgiveness in Christ. Even our dishonesty and repeated failures are not too big for him to forgive.

TODAY'S LESSON

It may have been hard for you this week to admit your sin, ask God to forgive you, and repent. One reason is that we secretly like our sin. Our sin <u>feels good</u> to us while we're doing it. This is because there are things in our lives that we love, trust, or fear more than God. The Bible calls these things IDOLS.

Does the idea of worshiping idols sound silly to you? Well, people who worship idols made of wood and stone have their reasons—some of them not so silly! And *you* have reasons why you're tempted to worship your own kind of idols, too.

Yes, this lesson is about *your* idols.

❑ First, you'll learn why people in Bible times worshiped *their* idols.

❑ Second, you'll find out what some of *your* idols are.

❑ Third, you'll see why Jesus is better than any idols—even yours.

PART 1: WHY WOULD ANYONE WORSHIP AN IDOL?

(25 minutes for the longer class option, or 15 minutes for the shorter class option)

Let's learn about idols in Bible times. Read what some idol worshipers have to say, and answer the questions.

Idol:
BAAL

Date:
870 BC

Place:
SIDON,
PHOENECIA

"I worship Baal because I'm a farmer and we need rain to grow food and survive. Baal wakes up every fall and sends thunderstorms. He throws lightning bolts and makes it pour rain!

It's important that I worship Baal by giving him sacrifices. I also help wake him up every year by joining wild parties at his temple. The parties give him energy to wake up and send rain. The priests at the temple cut themselves with swords too. All their gushing blood helps get Baal's attention.

I need to please Baal because without his rain we'd die. Plus, I enjoy the wild parties. They're naughty fun!"

What does the worshiper <u>love</u> about Baal?

Wild parties

How does he <u>trust</u> Baal to care for him?

Sending rain

What does he <u>fear</u> that makes him worship Baal?

Starvation and death

Idol: Date: Place:
ATHENA   49 AD   Athens, Greece

"We Greeks worship many gods. They all have temples here in Athens. My favorite goddess, Athena, stands for wisdom, happy home life, and solid families.

I take great pride in my city. Our devotion to Athena and wisdom makes us the smartest people in the world. Philosophers everywhere look up to us. I serve Athena by studying wisdom. I also bring gifts to her temple, the Parthenon. Worshiping her keeps my family life happy.

I keep this up because I wouldn't want her to feel neglected. She can get grumpy, you know. If I don't worship her, she might do something mean to disrupt my happy home life."

What does the worshiper <u>love</u> about Athena?

Pride in being wise and respected

How does she <u>trust</u> Athena to care for her?

Gives a happy home life

What does she <u>fear</u> that makes her worship Athena?

Appearing unwise, disruptions to family life

TALK ABOUT IT

Now discuss what you learned about idol worship. Even though Baal worshipers and Athena worshipers want very different things, how are the worship of Baal and Athena similar?

Help students to see that in each case the worshiper (1) <u>loves</u> something about the idol or what that idol offers, (2) <u>trusts</u> the idol to take care of him or her, and (3) <u>fears</u> things that drive him or her to worship the idol.

OPTIONAL DISCUSSION IF YOU HAVE TIME: If you have a long class session and don't usually divide lessons, spend more time discussing love, trust, and fear.

- ★ *Read together* **Psalm 18:1–3***.*
- ★ *On a whiteboard, write LOVE, TRUST, FEAR.*
- ★ *Ask: Whom does Psalm 18 say we should love? Whom does it say we should trust? Whom does it say will save us from what we fear?*
- ★ *Ask: How well do you think you really love, trust, and depend on God when you're afraid more than people who worshiped Baal and Athena did?*

HAVING IDOLS IS ABOUT:

1. what you <u>love (instead of God)</u>

2. what you <u>trust (instead of God)</u>

3. what you <u>fear (instead of believing God will protect you)</u>

Now learn what God thinks of idols and worship. Draw a line from each statement below to a phrase in the Bible that tells about it.

- ❏ An idol can be *anything* in the world that takes your worship.

- ❏ An idol is something you make for yourself to control your own life—instead of letting God be in control.

- ❏ Anything you're greedy for and want more than you want God is an idol.

- ❏ God HATES idols. He's jealous for your worship.

"You shall not make for yourself a carved image, or any likeness of anything that is in heaven above, or that is in the earth beneath, or that is in the water under the earth. You shall not bow down to them or serve them, for I the LORD your God am a jealous God." (Exodus 20:4–5)

Put to death, therefore . . . greed, which is idolatry. (Colossians 3:5 NIV)

PART 2: WHAT IDOLS MIGHT *YOU* WORSHIP?

(20 minutes)

You probably don't worship Baal or Athena, but anything you <u>love</u> more than God, <u>trust</u> more than God, or <u>fear losing</u> more than God is *an idol to you.*

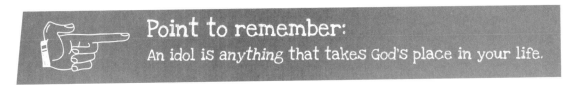

> **Point to remember:**
> An idol is *anything* that takes God's place in your life.

Here are some examples.

- ❑ 🖤 Draw a **heart** next to the sentence that shows what the student <u>loves</u>.

- ❑ ★ Draw a **star** next to the sentence that shows what the student <u>trusts</u>.

- ❑ 💧 Draw a **drop of sweat** next to the sentence that shows what the student <u>fears</u>.

Idol: MONEY

"I dream about being able to buy anything I want."
(Love)

"I feel safe because I know my parents have plenty of money."
(Trust)

"Being poor would be the worst!"
(Fear)

Spend a few minutes thinking about what your own idols might be. To identify your idols, consider what you daydream about, or what makes you angry if you don't get it. Now check those things in this list that are idols in YOUR life. What do you love, trust, or fear not having more than God?

_____ Being first or important

_____ Being popular with friends

_____ Success in school

_____ Success in sports

_____ Success in _____

_____ Approval of parents

_____ Approval of teachers

_____ Approval of _____

_____ Money

_____ Movies or TV

_____ Video games or toys

_____ Family

_____ Being noticed or famous

_____ Good looks (or not looking dorky)

_____ Never being laughed at

_____ Being thought of as smart

_____ Long life and health

_____ Acceptance by others

_____ Being included in fun things

_____ Getting my fair share

_____ Being talented

_____ Good reputation

_____ Comfortable life

_____ Recognition for what I'm good at

TALK ABOUT IT

Some things in the list are good things, aren't they? But if you love, trust, or fear not having them more than you do God, they're still dangerous idols—even more dangerous because they look like good things!

Share with the group what some of your most dangerous idols are. Tell what you do that shows they're idols in your life.

It's important to get students to name and acknowledge some of their idols. This is a necessary first step in repenting of those idols. If students have trouble at this point identifying behavior that stems from their idols, that's okay. Encourage them to move on to the next exercise, and show them the example below.

SHARING OPPORTUNITY: You as the leader need to participate in this exercise and the one about idol-worshiping behavior below. Let your students see that it's okay to admit our idols so we can repent and fight the sin they lead us into. Repentance is a godly activity and one that shows growth in a believer's life, not one that represents failure.

Now choose one idol from those you checked on the last page. Pick one that's especially tempting to you. Draw a picture of it as if it were a Bible-times statue kind of idol. Also draw a picture of yourself, the idol worshiper, explaining how you serve that idol.

Example: *If your idol is being smart or looking smart to others, you might draw a statue holding textbooks and wearing nerdy glasses. Then you might write one of the following:*

❑   I love <u>looking smart</u>, so I <u>show off how much I know</u>.

❑   I trust <u>being smart</u>, so I <u>study hard because it'll make me successful</u>.

❑   I fear <u>people thinking I'm stupid</u>, so I <u>can't stand when they think I don't know something</u>.

Help students to see that our idols end up controlling our lives. What we idolize results in behavior that's an alternative to loving and trusting God.

PART 3: WHAT'S BETTER THAN IDOLS?

(15 minutes)

Serving idols is like drinking seawater. If you were adrift in a lifeboat with nothing but seawater around you, drinking it would feel good at first. But soon that salty water would kill you.

It's the same with your idols. It feels good to serve them. Often it feels like you just *have* to serve them. But they're deadly. They can't really satisfy you.

❑ ONLY the living God is worth your love.

❑ ONLY the living God is always trustworthy.

❑ ONLY the living God can conquer what you fear.

❑ ONLY Jesus is the living water—fresh water that quenches your thirst.

The apostle Paul preached in Athens once. He spoke right next to the temple where people worshiped the idol Athena. Read what he said about the true God.

The God who made the world and everything in it, being Lord of heaven and earth, does not live in temples made by man, nor is he served by human hands, as though he needed anything, since he himself gives to all mankind life and breath and everything. (Acts 17:24–25)

<u>Underline</u> at least three things that make the true God better than Athena.

Put a star next to the one thing that you're most thankful is true about God.

Students might notice that God:

* ★ *Made the world*
* ★ *Is Lord of everything*
* ★ *Does not live in manmade temples*
* ★ *Doesn't need us to serve him*
* ★ *Doesn't need anything*
* ★ *Gives us life and everything else*

Emphasize how Athena, like all idols, is mostly about requiring service from her worshipers. But the true God is all about giving to us, not taking from us.

God sent someone to speak to Baal worshipers too. The prophet Elijah had a contest with the priests of Baal to see whether Baal or the true God could send lightning and rain. Nothing happened when Baal's priests yelled and cut themselves and made their blood flow. But when Elijah prayed to the true God, he sent fire from heaven.

Read what Elijah said in his prayer.

> *O LORD, answer me, so these people may know that you, O LORD, are God, and that you are turning their hearts back again. (1 Kings 18:37 NIV)*

<u>Underline</u> the two things Elijah prayed for the people to know about God.

What does God do for the hearts of his people?

He turns their hearts from idols, back to himself.

 Elijah prayed that the people would know (1) that the Lord is God and (2) that he is turning their hearts back to him. Emphasize how we can return to God when we catch ourselves worshiping idols. He has done much for us to make our hearts eager to return to him!

Your idolatry is very bad, but you can turn back to Jesus. He's not at all like idols!

- ❑ Idols have no real power, but Jesus does.

- ❑ Idols promise that you can earn happiness by being devoted to them, but Jesus saves us for free.

- ❑ Idols are harsh. Baal's priests cut themselves trying to serve him. But Jesus bled for us! Serving him is joyful thanksgiving, not harsh duty.

End by praying to the true God. Your prayer should have two parts:

1. **Thanks.** Even though you struggle with many idols, be thankful that Jesus died for you—an idol worshiper! Thank him that Jesus bled for you. Also praise him for whatever you put a star next to in Paul's sermon at Athens.

2. **Request.** Ask God to turn your heart away from the idols in your life and back to him. Look back at the things you checked as idols in your life. Pray about each one, asking God to turn your heart away from it.

 A lesson on idols can be convicting. It's important that students take time not only to see how Jesus is better than idols, but also to engage the fight against idols in their lives by working together with the Spirit. Prayer, therefore, is essential. Encourage students to be honest with God about the idols in their lives and to look in faith to him to more fully win over their hearts. Urge them to pray for this often—every time they feel themselves tempted to give in to an idol.

MAKE IT STICK:

NOTICE YOUR IDOL WORSHIP

(Take 5 minutes at the end of the session to explain the coming week's "Make It Stick" exercise.)

INSTRUCTIONS:

☐ Fill out this Make It Stick page during the week.

☐ Don't forget to bring your *Student Guide* back next time you meet.

☐ If you have time, go ahead and get started now.

It's important to notice idols in your life so you can repent of them and act more like the holy person God has made you. On the line below, write one idol that's especially tempting to you. (If you like, also draw a picture of what an actual stone or wooden idol of what you worship might look like.)

At the end of each day in the coming week, think of something specific you did that day because of the idol you mentioned above. Write the specific thing you did on the line below.

DAY ONE
What I did today because of my idol: _____

DAY TWO
What I did today because of my idol: _____

DAY THREE
What I did today because of my idol: _____

DAY FOUR
What I did today because of my idol: _____

DAY FIVE
What I did today because of my idol: _____

DAY SIX
What I did today because of my idol: _____

DAY SEVEN
What I did today because of my idol: _____

Because idol worship is sin, pray to God when you write down your behavior.

Ask him to forgive your sin.

Thank him that you may turn back to him again and again—every time you catch yourself worshiping an idol—and *always* be forgiven!

Ask him to turn your heart away from that idol and toward him.

Praise him for how he's better than that idol.

LOOK! SHARK!

Big Idea: Confronting Unbelief

NOTES TO THE LEADER

LESSON GOAL

Students will learn to look below surface-level sins and see the unbelief of the heart. They will start identifying heart-level unbelief in their own hearts, and be encouraged that God fights that sin alongside them.

SUMMARY

This lesson picks up where the previous lesson about idols left off. Your students have learned that identifying <u>idols</u> is one way to take a deeper look at their sin. Now they'll look still deeper to see their <u>unbelief</u>. The lesson uses the example of a shark, hidden under the water with only its fin showing, to explain how hidden unbelief produces the surface-level sins we can see.

PART ONE will be a study of two examples of liars in the Bible: Abram, and Ananias and Sapphira. Your students will see how Abram failed to believe God's promises to him . . . which led to fear of being killed (his idol) . . . which led to his lying. They'll see how Ananias and Sapphira failed to believe Jesus was better than a good reputation in the church . . . which led to a desire to look generous (their idol) . . . which led to their lying.

In PART TWO, your students will apply this method of "looking under the surface" to their own lives. Using the shark figure, they'll look beneath their surface sins and consider how they need to believe the gospel more deeply.

PART THREE is encouragement that Christ lives in your students' hearts by faith, and that he fights alongside them to help them believe in him more deeply and battle sin in their lives. Once again, you and your students will end by practicing deeper belief, through prayer.

YOUR PREPARATION

STUDY. Read the lesson, including the Bible accounts of Abram and of Ananias and Sapphira, and become familiar with how the Shark Figure works. Be prepared to explain how believing the gospel of Jesus is a fundamental activity for a Christian, and one on which all growth in holiness rests. Jesus said, "This is the work of God, that you believe in him whom he has sent" (John 6:29).

BE READY TO SHARE. The Shark Figure provides an opportunity for your students to consider their surface sins, their idols, and the unbelief beneath it all. You need to fill out the figure alongside your students. Decide beforehand what you'll share about your own sin, idols, and unbelief. It's best to pick an area of your life where you also see some growth due to how you've learned to believe the gospel more deeply. That way, you can encourage your students with how deeper belief has helped you to fight sin. You can give God credit and speak about the value of believing the gospel, which is better than merely confessing sin. You can look to Jesus, which is necessary in a lesson like this one that includes much looking at ourselves.

PRAY. Start praying now about what example from your life you should share with your students. Ask God to show you a good example of how deeper belief in the gospel has led to victory over sin. For your students, pray the prayer from Ephesians 3:14–19 that's used in part 3 of this lesson—asking God to increase their knowledge of the love of Christ.

BEFORE YOU BEGIN

(About 10 minutes)

Share some of the ways you caught yourself serving an idol in your life. What did you learn about how your sin is connected to idols deep in your heart?

Do you think your sin is mostly connected to:

- Something you <u>love</u> more than you love God,

- Something you <u>trust</u> more than you trust God, or

- Something you <u>fear</u> instead of trusting God?

Encourage students to share. It may help for you to begin by sharing some personal observations about idols that tempt you and how this affects your behavior. Emphasize the connection between idols and sinful behavior. That's the theme of today's lesson.

TODAY'S LESSON

Have you ever had someone tell you, "I have some good news and some bad news; which would you like to hear first?"? Which would you want to hear first: good news or bad?

Today's lesson starts with more bad news about your sin and idols. Sin is an even bigger, deeper problem than you may realize. You'll learn about it in three steps:

1. You'll look at two case studies of sinners in the Bible. You'll see how hidden sin, deep in their hearts, led them to sin outwardly.

2. You'll think about your own deep sins.

3. The good news! You'll see how to fight that deep sin by believing the gospel.

It's all about how sin is like a shark, lurking under the surface of your life.

PART 1: SINNERS AND THE SHARK

(30 minutes)

Case Study 1:
Abram

Sins:

- **Lying**
- **Telling his wife to lie**
- **Giving up his wife while he got rich**

Abram was a man with much faith in God, but even he had idols. His story comes near the beginning of the Bible, and starts with God giving him great promises. <u>Underline</u> at least six things God told Abram he would do for him.

> *"I will make of you a great nation, and I will bless you and make your name great, so that you will be a blessing. I will bless those who bless you, and him who dishonors you I will curse, and in you all the families of the earth shall be blessed." (Genesis 12:2–3)*

Now read **Genesis 12:10–19** to see what Abram did shortly after that, then answer the questions below.

Abram told a huge lie and got lots of people in trouble! He sinned because there was an idol of fear in his life. What was he afraid of that led him to lie?

He was afraid he might be killed.

TALK ABOUT IT

What if Abram had more fully believed the promises God had told him earlier? Discuss how his trip to Egypt might have been different.

Allow students to speculate and discuss. Help them to see that if Abram had deeply believed God, he would have trusted that God would bless him and never let anyone kill him. Then he wouldn't have lied and wouldn't have lost Sarai to Pharaoh. He could have been a blessing to the Egyptians instead of causing trouble for them.

Think of sin as a shark. If you were swimming in the ocean and saw a large fin sticking out of the water, would you just ignore it? No! You'd know there was something more dangerous lurking under the surface—a shark! Our sin is like that. The sins we can see tell us there's something even more dangerous under the surface, inside our hearts, that's making us sin.

Let's see how that worked with Abram. On the line above the water, near the shark fin, write "lying." That's how Abram sinned in Egypt.

Sin you can see:

Lying

The idol under the sin:

Abram had love / trust / fear of:

being killed

The deepest sin of all—UNBELIEF:

Abram didn't really believe God, that:

He would bless him like he promised

Under the water, near the shark, circle how Abram's idol that caused him to do the sins we could see was a "fear" idol. He was scared he might be killed. So write "being killed" on the second line.

But the biggest, deepest sin lurking in Abram's heart was **unbelief**:

Question:

Why did Abram sin?

Answer:

He **feared** he might be killed.

Question:

But *why* did he fear?

Answer:

Because he **didn't fully believe** God would bless him and keep him alive to become a great nation like God had promised.

So on the bottom line write "he would bless him like he promised." That was Abram's unbelief.

Point to remember:
Not believing God is the big, deep, dangerous sin that leads to all the others.

You may have to explain the shark diagram a few times before students understand the connection between surface-level sins and deeper, heart-level sins. If necessary, take time to explain again how Abram's failure to believe God led to all his problems and sin. When students understand, you're ready to move on to the second case study.

Case Study 2:
Ananias and Sapphira

Sins:

- **Lying**
- **Pretending to be generous**

Ananias and Sapphira were part of the church in Jerusalem not long after Jesus lived on earth. The people in that church loved belonging to Jesus so much that they shared everything they owned with each other. One man named Barnabus even sold an expensive field and gave all the money to the apostles to help needy people in the church. That was impressive! Ananias and Sapphira decided they wanted to look impressive too. Read **Acts 5:1–10** to see what happened.

TALK ABOUT IT

Ananias and Sapphira pretended to give all the money they got to the church so they would look good, like Barnabas. Discuss what you think their idols were. Think of several things.

Ananias and Sapphira probably loved a good reputation. Maybe they loved being famous in the church. Perhaps they loved attention and couldn't stand for Barnabas to get more attention in the church than they did. They also might have put their trust in having a certain amount of money available that they could fall back on. All of these are possible idols in their lives.

Now use the shark to understand Ananias and Sapphira's sin. For the sin you can see, write "lying and pretending."

Sin you can see:

Lying and pretending

The idol under the sin:

Ananias & Sapphira had love / trust / fear of:

A good reputation in the church

The deepest sin of all—UNBELIEF:

Ananias & Sapphira didn't really believe God, that:

Jesus is better than being popular and gives us all we need

The Bible doesn't say what Ananias and Sapphira were thinking, so we have to guess what their idol was. Maybe one idol was that they trusted money and wanted to keep some in case of emergencies. Their biggest idol, though, seems to be that they loved being famous and popular and having a good reputation in the church. So circle love and then write "a good reputation in the church" on the line for their idol.

But as always, the biggest, deepest sin lurking in their hearts was **unbelief**.

Question:

Why did Ananias and Sapphira sin?

Answer:

They **loved** having a good reputation in the church.

Question:

But *why* did they love a good reputation?

Answer:

Because they **didn't fully believe** that just belonging to Jesus and serving him is far better than being famous and popular. He gives *everything* good we need.

So on the bottom line write "Jesus is better than being popular and gives us all we need."

The unbelief may be somewhat less obvious in this example. Take time to discuss it with your students and make sure they understand it. Students need to see how God has promised that nothing is better than Jesus and that we have all we need in him. These are critical promises to believe if we are to overcome idols of love and trust. Ananias and Sapphira appear to have failed to believe this. They never would have lied to earn a good reputation if they truly believed Jesus was better.

PART 2: YOU AND THE SHARK

(25 minutes)

Read **Mark 7:21–23** to learn what Jesus said about where our sin comes from. Write the answer below.

Jesus says our sin comes

from within, out of the heart

Jesus agrees you have a shark under the surface—a big sin problem deep inside you. Because sin comes from your heart, just trying not to sin or staying away from bad influences won't stop your sin. You have a heart problem. When you sin, something other than Jesus has become more important to your heart. You need to believe more deeply that Jesus is better.

Look at some examples of how that might work, using the shark:

My Sin you can See:

telling lies

My idol under this sin:

I had love / trust / (fear) of:
(circle one)

people might think less of me if they knew the truth

I don't really believe God, that:

he thinks the world of me no matter what I'm like

What other people think of me has become more important to my heart than the good news.

My Sin you can See:

taking the biggest piece of cake or pizza

My idol under this sin:

I had (love) / trust / fear of:
(circle one)

always being greedy to have the most or best for myself

I don't really believe God, that:

in Jesus he gives me all I need, and so much heavenly blessing-so I can easily let others have the best worldly things

Worldly things have become more important to my heart than this good news.

Now practice with some of your own sins. Pick some outward sins you do often. Then fill in what they show about the shark in your heart.

My sin you can see:

My idol under this sin:

I had love / trust / fear of:
(circle one)

I don't really believe God, that:

My sin you can see:

My idol under this sin:

I had love / trust / fear of:
(circle one)

I don't really believe God, that:

TALK ABOUT IT

Discuss what you wrote. If necessary, ask others in the group to help you understand what about Jesus you fail to believe.

It's likely that some students will need guidance completing this figure, especially in seeing what their unbelief is.

- ★ *If they have LOVE idols, suggest they think about what makes Jesus more love-worthy . . . and believe it!*

- ★ *If they have TRUST idols, suggest they think about what Jesus gives us and how he cares for us . . . and believe it!*

- ★ *If they have FEAR idols, suggest they think about how Jesus protects us . . . and believe it!*

SHARING OPPORTUNITY: Complete a Shark Figure for yourself alongside your students. Share with them how you sin, what idols this reveals in your life, and how you need to believe better. It will help if you can provide some encouragement by also sharing how God has helped you grow, strengthening your belief and resulting in a stronger fight against sin in your life.

"This could get depressing. My sin problem goes so deep I have no chance at all of fixing it!"

"It's true that you can't fix it. But God's Spirit changes hearts! He helps us to believe."

PART 3: SHOOTING THE SHARK

(20 minutes)

You wouldn't hunt a shark by shooting at its fin. You'd aim at the shark's body under the water. In the same way, the most important part of fighting sin is to aim at your heart. You need to aim deep. Start by believing how much Jesus loves you.

READ WHAT PAUL WROTE IN THE BOOK OF EPHESIANS.

> *For this reason I kneel before the Father, from whom his whole family in heaven and on earth derives its name. I pray that out of his glorious riches he may strengthen you with power through his Spirit in your inner being, so that Christ may dwell in your hearts through faith. And I pray that you, being rooted and established in love, may have power, together with all the saints, to grasp how wide and long and high and deep is the love of Christ, and to know this love that surpasses knowledge. (Ephesians 3:14–19 NIV)*

Where does the Spirit work to strengthen you with power?

The inner being

In what part of you does Christ dwell?

The heart

What does God's work in you give you power to grasp (understand)?

How wide and long and high and deep is the love of Christ.

If you're joined to Jesus, you CAN fight your sin—successfully! You can *shoot that shark*, because God's Spirit is in your heart, changing you on the inside, helping you to know and believe his love more deeply.

Finish by praying, like Paul did. Pray two things:

1. Thank God for the many, many ways he loves you and cares for you. Mention some that have come up in this lesson or in other recent lessons. Make a list here of ways God is kind to you, and refer to it when you pray.

   _____

   _____

   _____

   _____

2. Ask God to help you believe that everything he says about his love for you is true. Pray that you will know "how wide and long and high and deep is the love of Christ"—and will believe it!

Don't rush through this prayer. After taking a deep look at our sin, it's important to take a deep look at Jesus too. Make sure your students dwell on his goodness to them. Help them to leave encouraged that, although they struggle with sins of the heart, they have a God who changes hearts fighting alongside them.

Both outward repentance and change in the heart can be frustratingly slow at times. Your students may need to be encouraged that trusting God more fully is the right response when their fight against sin doesn't seem to be making progress. He will change them in his good time. They need to remain in him, trusting and believing Jesus as they struggle to grow (John 15:4–5). Such deeper faith is itself progress.

MAKE IT STICK:
THE SHARK CHART

(Take 5 minutes at the end of the session to explain the coming week's "Make It Stick" exercise.)

INSTRUCTIONS:

❑ Fill out this Make It Stick page during the week.

❑ Don't forget to bring your *Student Guide* back next time you meet.

❑ If you have time, go ahead and get started now.

Use the Shark Chart to keep a record of some of the sins in your life. As you catch yourself having sinned:

1. Write down the sin.

2. Then figure out what's the idol "under the surface."

3. Then write down what you failed to believe about Jesus.

Remember always to pray as you think about your sin. Ask God to forgive you (he surely will!) and to help your heart to believe. The Holy Spirit fights that shark right alongside you!

THE SHARK CHART

what sins are lurking under the surface?

MY SIN YOU CAN SEE: | MY SIN YOU CAN SEE: | MY SIN YOU CAN SEE:

_____

MY IDOL
UNDER THIS SIN:

I have **LOVE / TRUST / FEAR** of:
(CIRCLE ONE)

_____

I DON'T REALLY
BELIEVE GOD, THAT:

MY IDOL
UNDER THIS SIN:

I have **LOVE / TRUST / FEAR** of:
(CIRCLE ONE)

_____

I DON'T REALLY
BELIEVE GOD, THAT:

MY IDOL
UNDER THIS SIN:

I have **LOVE / TRUST / FEAR** of:
(CIRCLE ONE)

_____

I DON'T REALLY
BELIEVE GOD, THAT:

As you note your sin, remember that **IN JESUS YOU HAVE FORGIVENESS,** and that
HIS SPIRIT WILL WORK IN YOUR HEART to fix the big sin and the unbelief that lurks under the surface.
Use your time filling out this page as a time of confession and prayer.

LESSON 10

THAT'S MY DAD!

Big Idea: Living as God's Child

NOTES TO THE LEADER

LESSON GOAL

Students will gain a greater appreciation for how believers are sons and daughters of God, the King. They will recognize behavior in their lives that's son-like and behavior that's orphan-like, and be challenged to live like children of God.

SUMMARY

This is the last lesson in our unit that looks at the underlying motives of the heart. In this lesson, your students will learn how a deep confidence that they are children of God creates a heart that's unselfish, willing to be corrected, and unafraid to live for God.

PART ONE will be a study of the story of King David and his kindness toward Mephibosheth. Your students will learn how Mephibosheth went from being an orphaned enemy of David to being treated like the king's adopted son. It's a picture of how God adopts believers.

PART TWO will teach the benefits of being a child of God. His children receive CARE, an INHERITANCE, LOVE, and HONOR.

PART THREE will give your students a chance to think about the difference between the way an orphan behaves and the way a child of God behaves—when that child deeply believes God is his loving Father. You and your students will discuss how joy and confidence in our adoption makes a difference in daily behavior. Your prayer today will celebrate the blessings of adoption and thank God for them.

YOUR PREPARATION

STUDY. Read through the lesson and the descriptions of orphan and son/daughter behavior so that you're ready to discuss these with your students. Also learn the Mephibosheth story from the Bible. There are three Bible passages that make up that story:

★ *2 Samuel 9*

★ *2 Samuel 16:1–4 (as David flees Jerusalem with his court during an uprising)*

★ *2 Samuel 19:24–30 (as David returns home)*

You should read all parts of the Bible story and be familiar with it. For this lesson's purposes, understanding David's somewhat puzzling behavior at the end of the story is not really important. Mephibosheth's response to being treated as a son is what matters.

BE READY TO SHARE. You need to come prepared with a specific example of how knowing you're a child of God makes a difference in some everyday behavior in your life. Look through the list of orphan and son/ daughter behaviors for ideas, and be ready to share when discussing the list with your students.

PRAY. Pray that God would enlarge your own appreciation of being a child of the King, and that your excitement over this would show as you lead your students through this lesson.

BEFORE YOU BEGIN

(10 minutes)

Share something you learned about your sin this week.

What was a surface-level sin? _____

What idol in your life caused you to sin that way? _____

Your idol means there was something about Jesus you didn't believe.

What did you **not believe**?

_____

_____

_____

Did you experience any growth? By seeing your unbelief and praying about it, were you able to believe more deeply? Share about this.

Use this time to review, making sure to celebrate God's grace wherever a student has a positive report. Remind students about the connection between surface sins, idols, and unbelief. Many students have a hard time understanding what it is they fail to believe. You can encourage them that today's lesson will teach more good news about Jesus to believe—which will help in fighting sin.

TODAY'S LESSON

Sometimes it's hard to believe that Jesus is *so good* to you. It helps to remember that God is a great King and Jesus makes you the King's child.

Imagine a good and powerful king who rules a vast kingdom. He reigns from the largest, most dazzling castle in the world. For most people, just to visit that castle would be a breathtaking honor. To actually meet the king once and speak to him would fulfill the dream of a lifetime. To become his trusted advisor is impossible.

It'll never happen.

But YOU are the king's child. He loves you with all his heart. You spend time with him whenever you want. For meals, you sit next to him in the castle's great banquet hall, eating at his table and talking with him about every need of the kingdom.

What <u>HONOR</u> is yours!

What <u>INFLUENCE</u> you have in the kingdom!

What <u>POWER</u> you have to do good in the world!

What <u>CONFIDENCE</u> you enjoy!

Best of all, what <u>LOVE</u> and <u>APPROVAL</u> you feel from the king himself, your dad!

In this lesson, you'll see how a believer's life with God is like that story.

PART 1: THE ORPHAN AND THE KING

(15 minutes)

Let's begin by learning about an orphan and a king in the Bible. First, meet the characters.

The King:
David

New king of Israel, living in a palace in Jerusalem

Became king after being hunted by the old king, Saul

Godly man who was friends with Saul's son, Jonathan, even though Saul was his enemy

- - - - - - - - - - - - - - - - - - -

The Orphan:
Mephibosheth (Meh-FIB-oh-Sheth)

Grandson of Saul, living in disgrace in Lo-debar, on the outskirts of Israel

Crippled as a child when he fled the palace after his father and Saul were killed in battle

One of the few surviving members of the family of Saul, David's old enemy

Now read the story.

And David said, "Is there still anyone left of the house of Saul, that I may show him kindness for Jonathan's sake?"

Now there was a servant of the house of Saul whose name was Ziba, and they called him to David. Ziba said to the king, "There is still a son of Jonathan; he is crippled in his feet."

The king said to him, "Where is he?"

And Ziba said to the king, "He is in the house of Machir the son of Ammiel, at Lo-debar."

Then King David sent and brought him. And Mephibosheth the son of Jonathan, son of Saul, came to David and fell on his face and paid homage.

And David said, "Mephibosheth!"

And he answered, "Behold, I am your servant."

And David said to him, "Do not fear, for I will show you kindness for the sake of your father Jonathan, and I will restore to you all the land of Saul, and you shall eat at my table always."

Then the king called Ziba, Saul's servant, and said to him, "All that belonged to Saul and to all his house I have given to your master's grandson. And you and your sons and your servants shall till the land for him and shall bring in the produce, that your master's grandson may have bread to eat. But Mephibosheth your master's grandson shall always eat at my table."

So Mephibosheth ate at David's table, like one of the king's sons. And all who lived in Ziba's house became Mephibosheth's servants. So Mephibosheth lived in Jerusalem, for he ate always at the king's table. (excerpted from 2 Samuel 9)

How much did Mephibosheth <u>deserve</u> for David to be kind to him?

☐	☐	☐	☐	☐
Not at all	Only a little	Somewhat	Quite a bit	He totally earned it!

How great was David's kindness to Mephibosheth?

☐	☐	☐	☐	☐
Barely kind at all	A little bit kind	Somewhat kind	Very kind	Incredibly kind!

TALK ABOUT IT

How do you think Mephibosheth felt at the end of the story compared to how he felt at the beginning?

Why do you think the Bible mentions *four times* how David let Mephibosheth always eat at the king's table? What's so important about that?

Make sure students see three points:

★ *Mephibosheth didn't deserve any kindness at all from David, yet received incredible kindness.*

★ *Mephibosheth was a potential enemy of David, yet received kindness. He must have been scared at first and grateful later.*

★ *The king's table was a place of honor and acceptance, a sign that Mephibosheth was treated "like one of the king's sons." He went from being an orphan to being like the son of the king.*

PART 2: YOUR FATHER THE KING

(20 minutes)

Mephibosheth was an orphan (his father had died). Then David—the king himself!—became like a father to him. That's a picture of what happens to you when you believe in Jesus. Even though you don't deserve it and have been a God-hating sinner, God <u>adopts you</u> as his child.

Look up the following verses in your Bible and fill in the blanks.

Galatians 3:26

For in

<u>Christ Jesus</u>

you are all

<u>sons of God</u> through faith.

John 1:12

But to all who did

<u>receive him,</u> who

<u>believed in his name</u>, he gave the right to become

<u>children of God</u>.

The story of the good and powerful king who's your dad isn't just a fairy tale to imagine. It's all true! When God saves you, he does more than just forgive your sin and count you righteous. He also makes you his own son or daughter.

The list below includes some of the benefits of being a son or daughter. Next to each Bible verse, write the benefit it describes (some might describe more than one).

BENEFITS OF DAUGHTERS AND SONS:

1. **CARE:** Your father takes care of you and protects you.

2. **INHERITANCE:** You get a share of everything your father owns.

3. **LOVE:** Your father accepts you, enjoys spending time with you and listens to you.

4. **HONOR:** You share your father's name and reputation

Benefit

inheritance

love

love/care

care

inheritance

love/care

love/honor

inheritance/care

Verse

You are no longer a slave, but a son, and if a son, then an heir through God. (Galatians 4:7)

We know that he hears us in whatever we ask. (1 John 5:15)

Let us then with confidence draw near to the throne of grace, that we may receive mercy and find grace to help in time of need. (Hebrews 4:16)

Casting all your anxieties on him, because he cares for you. (1 Peter 5:7)

Blessed are the meek, for they shall inherit the earth. (Matthew 5:5)

Who shall separate us from the love of Christ? Shall tribulation, or distress, or persecution, or famine, or nakedness, or danger, or sword? (Romans 8:35)

See what kind of love the Father has given to us, that we should be called children of God; and so we are. (1 John 3:1)

Let no one boast in men, for all things are yours. (1 Corinthians 3:21)

It isn't important that students get the "right answers" in these blanks. Each verse shows many aspects of God's fatherly character, and the answers could be arranged several ways. The point is that students read the verses and think about how they show God to be a good Father.

TALK ABOUT IT

What are some ways that being a child of God ought to feel a lot like the story from the beginning of this lesson about you being a king's child? How would you compare it to that?

Help students to see that being a child of God is very similar. In fact, being God's child means even better love and care and even greater inheritance and honor because God is a perfect Father and the greatest King of all! We just don't really recognize sometimes all we have as his children.

OPTIONAL STOPPING POINT

If you're dividing this lesson into two class sessions, take a break here.

If you're stopping the lesson here for today, send your students home with *something to think about* and *prayer*.

SOMETHING TO THINK ABOUT

One of the most amazing blessings of our salvation is our adoption into God's family. We now are the children of the living God and have all the benefits and privileges as sons and daughters.

Think back to today's lesson of King David and Mephibosheth. How are you like Mephibosheth now that you have been adopted into God's family?

Let students start answering in class and write a few answers down on a whiteboard. Then send students home for the week to think of still more ways they're like Mephibosheth, with a promise that they can add those to the list next week. How does this knowledge (belief) change the way we react to our fears, worries, and lack of love for others?

PRAYER

Pray through the list of Bible verses above that mention the benefits of being a son or daughter of God. Let students take turns thanking God for one or two of the many blessings mentioned in those verses.

When you restart this lesson later, begin with *review*.

REVIEW

Remind the students of the story of King David and his kindness toward Mephibosheth. Let them tell you about the characters and what happened, being sure to cover the following points:

★ *Mephibosheth didn't deserve any kindness at all from David and was a potential enemy, yet he received incredible kindness.*

★ *The king's table was a place of honor and acceptance, a sign that Mephibosheth was treated "like one of the king's sons." He went from being an orphan to being like the son of the king.*

Ask the student: How is your story of salvation like the story of King David and Mephibosheth? Answers might include:

★ *We were God's enemies, but he made us his children.*

★ *God gives kindness we don't deserve.*

★ *We were helpless, but God saved us.*

★ *We sit at God's table.*

★ *God gives us honor/care/an inheritance.*

PART 3: LIVING LIKE A DAUGHTER OR SON

(40 minutes. Be sure to leave time for each student to pray at the end of this part of the lesson)

Let's compare an orphan with a child who has parents.

Orphan

Child who has parents

DISCUSS.

Which will be more scared? Why?

Which will worry about having to take care of himself? Why?

Which will always be trying to get people to like her? Why?

Make sure students understand that an orphan is insecure. An orphan must trust in him/herself because an orphan has no father to rely on. An orphan must also work hard to get people to like him/her, or else no one will show the orphan kindness.

If you're joined to Jesus, God always loves you—even when you don't deserve it—because ★ you're his child. But if you forget this *you* might start to act like an orphan.

- ❏ You might act scared.

- ❏ You might act like you need to look out for your own interests.

- ❏ You might act like you need to make people like you.

Each of these students has two ways they can think. One is "orphan thinking." The other is thinking like a son or daughter. For each student, put an X through the orphan thinking.

TALK ★ ABOUT IT

Look back at the past several pages and think more about the ways a son or daughter will act. Tell which of those examples are the hardest for you. (Circle) some orphan statements that sound like the way you often talk or think.

There's a responsibility that comes with being a child of the King. You need to act like your Dad. The Bible says those who are God's children keep his commandments, and "by this it is evident who are the children of God" (1 John 3:10). How much do you think you look and act like a child of God?

Imagine you absolutely believed everything the Bible tells you about being a child of the King. How would your thinking and your behavior be more like a daughter or son . . .

> . . . at home?

> . . . at school?

> . . . at church?

> . . . with your friends?

Help students really read and think about the individual orphan and son/daughter statements by making sure they circle some that especially apply to them. You may need to ask more specific questions about situations in your students' lives to help them think of ways their behavior would change with less orphan thinking. As students share, help them to see how their belief makes a huge difference in their behavior. Show them what difference it makes when we fully believe the King is a good Father to us.

SHARING OPPORTUNITY: Give a specific example from your own life of how knowing you're a child of God makes a difference in your practical, everyday behavior. For example, you might tell about how it changes the way you treat certain other people . . . or how you handle criticism . . . or how you respond to disappointment. Make it specific.

Before you finish this lesson, you need to know about the end of the Mephibosheth story.

Years later, King David had to flee Jerusalem when enemies attacked. People thought Mephibosheth, as a member of Saul's family, would side with the enemies while David was gone. David even gave Mephibosheth's land to Ziba.

But when David returned, he found Mephibosheth had been so sad he hadn't even washed himself the whole time. Then Mephibosheth explained why he was so devoted to David: "All my grandfather's descendants deserved nothing but death from my lord the king, but you gave your servant a place among those who eat at your table" (2 Samuel 19:28 NIV).

Mephibosheth knew he was undeserving but was made a son! He was grateful. It changed his behavior. And when David offered to make Ziba give up the land again, Mephibosheth said, "Let him take everything, now that my lord the king has returned home safely" (v. 30 NIV).

Mephibosheth didn't care about what David could give him. He just loved David himself!

PRAY ABOUT IT

You can have that kind of love for your Father and King too. You need to sit at his table. You need to enjoy being his honored child.

Finish this lesson by turning back to the verses that tell the benefits of being a child of God. Take turns praying, thanking your Father for everything mentioned in those verses. Then ask him to help you believe they're all true!

Making this closing time of prayer a time of thanksgiving. Help students to focus on the verses and on thanking God for the sonship he gives them.

MAKE IT STICK:

THINK LIKE A SON OR DAUGHTER

(Take 5 minutes at the end of the session to explain the coming week's "Make It Stick" exercise.)

INSTRUCTIONS:

❑ Fill out this Make It Stick page during the week.
❑ Don't forget to bring your *Student Guide* back next time you meet.
❑ If you have time, go ahead and get started now.

This chart compares thinking like an orphan with thinking like a son or daughter. Read how an orphan thinks and then look up and read the verse that tells how a son or daughter of God thinks. In your own words, finish filling in the chart by writing how a son or daughter of God thinks.

HOW AN ORPHAN THINKS	WHAT GOD SAYS	HOW A SON OR DAUGHTER OF GOD THINKS
If only I could run faster, be taller, be thinner, or be as smart as he/she is, then I'd be accepted. It isn't fair!	John 1:12	My self-worth comes from . . . *being a child of God. God accepts me.*
I make sure I pray every day. It's the only way to keep God happy with me.	Psalm 16:11	I pray because . . . *I love my Father. Talking with him and trusting him is a joy.*
No one understands me and what I want. No one loves me.	1 John 4:16	I believe that . . . *God is my Father and he understands me perfectly. He made me and loves me.*
I go to church and pray and study the Bible but it's mostly so other people will see and approve.	Psalm 122:1	I go to church because . . . *I love to worship my Father.*
If I get good grades, or have good friends, or keep a good attitude my life will be better.	Psalm 84:11–12	God is in control of my life. I believe that he will . . . *give me good things. I will be blessed if I trust in him.*
I need to please everyone—my parents, my friends, my teachers . . .	1 Thessalonians 2:4	I can't please everyone. Instead I . . . *please God out of gratitude.*
God can't help me. I don't want to hear about him.	Isaiah 58:11	I trust that God can and will . . . *satisfy all my needs and make me strong.*
I must not fail! If I can't win I won't even try!	Philippians 4:12–13	It's okay to try and fail or to be weak. I can take it because . . . *I have an inward strength that comes from Jesus.*
People are always so mean! They pick on me. They aren't fair.	Philippians 4:6–8	People are mean (and I am too sometimes) but . . . *I tell God about it and enjoy his peace. I can focus on what's good.*
I don't like my house. I don't like my friends. I don't like my hair. I don't like my life . . .	Romans 8:28	I trust that God is . . . *filling my life with good things even when it's hard to see how they're good.*

When you finish, pick one place from the chart where you want to think less like an orphan and more like a son or daughter of God. Circle it. As you pray this week, thank God for how you're a daughter or son and ask him to help you to believe it and live like what you circled.

GRR...THAT MAKES ME SO MAD!

Big Idea: Resolving Conflicts

NOTES TO THE LEADER

LESSON GOAL

Students will learn how sinful desires of the heart often lead to conflict. They will learn and practice how thinking like a child of God gives the courage and ability to resolve conflicts with others.

SUMMARY

This lesson begins a unit in which your students will practice putting the gospel principles they've learned to work in their lives; repenting, forgiving, and (in this lesson) resolving conflicts. The account of Joseph and his conflict with his brothers provides the framework for this lesson. It also draws on the past two lessons—about under-the-surface sins and being a child of God.

PART ONE will examine how conflicts arise from sinful desires in the heart. These desires lead to jealously, greed, anger, pride, and other conflict-causing sins.

PART TWO will show how Joseph's life with God gave him the power to resolve his huge conflict:

★ Joseph dealt with his sin deeply by believing and trusting God—like your students learned to do with the shark example.

★ Joseph knew God had a good plan and was caring for him—like your students learned to see God as their Father.

You and your students will set the groundwork for doing the same with your own conflicts, using the confidence that comes from the gospel.

YOUR PREPARATION

STUDY. A large portion of Scripture is presented in condensed form in this lesson. You should become familiar with Joseph's entire life by reading Genesis 37; 39—45; and 50:15–21. Also meditate on James 4:1–2, which is the lesson's basis for the principle that conflicts arise from sinful desires in the heart. Knowing and having thought about these Scripture passages will let you add valuable insights as your students work through this lesson.

BE READY TO SHARE. In addition to talking about your own experience during the past week with the table of orphan and son/ daughter behaviors, you should be ready to share a specific example of a conflict you've had with someone and how your faith helped to resolve it. It may be that your sinful desires led to the conflict and you had to repent. Or it may be that someone else was unkind to you and you needed to forgive or to overcome evil with good. Either example will do, but your sharing will work best if you can tell how believing your status as a child of God made you willing and brave enough to deal with the conflict. It may take you a while to think of a fitting example to share, so start considering it now. Your chance to share will come near the end of this lesson.

PRAY. This lesson will end with you and your students being assigned to pray for a person they've had trouble getting along with. A great exercise for you, as the leader, would be to get a head start on that by beginning now to pray about conflicts in your life and to pray for your "enemies." Doing so should help you to come to this lesson with an eagerness to share with your students the joy of dealing with conflict.

BEFORE YOU BEGIN

(15 minutes)

From the last lesson share one place where you want to think less like an orphan and more like a son or daughter of God. Write that orphan thinking and son/daughter thinking on the lines below.

Orphan thinking _____

Son/daughter of God thinking _____

Share how you sometimes behave like an orphan. Then explain how it helps to believe that you're part of God's family. (HINT: Remember that God's children have <u>care</u>, an <u>inheritance</u>, <u>honor</u>, and <u>love</u> from God.)

> *Let students share and discuss. They may also want to talk about other orphan or son/daughter behaviors they noticed in themselves during the past week. You may want to review with them the principle behind orphan thinking vs. son/daughter thinking: Sons and daughters are confident and loving because they enjoy care, an inheritance, honor, and love from God.*

TODAY'S LESSON

Raise your hand if you've ever been in an argument with someone.

If you raised your hand, this lesson is for you. We're going to learn about arguments and conflicts. Let's start with a little quiz, just to see what you already think about conflicts.

Write TRUE or FALSE by each statement. Then discuss your answers, if you'd like.

_____ Conflicts start in my heart.

_____ I should treat others the same way they treat me.

_____ I should pray for those who are kind to me, but not for those who are mean to me.

_____ I need the Holy Spirit to help me love my enemies.

_____ I need to forgive others if I'm going to love them.

_____ I can overcome evil by being evil back.

_____ It's okay for me to pretend to be nice to someone, then talk badly about them behind their backs (they deserve it anyway—they're really mean!).

_____ Loving someone means I never have any conflict with them.

> *Don't worry about right and wrong answers in this opening exercise. Those will come at the end of this lesson. Use your time now as an opportunity to start thinking and talking about conflict.*

In this lesson, you'll start by learning where your conflicts come from. Then, in part 2, you'll see how being a child of God can help you solve conflicts.

PART 1: WHERE CONFLICTS COME FROM

(25 minutes)

Do you know the story of Joseph and his older brothers? Joseph's father loved him more than the others. God also gave Joseph dreams that said he'd become great. The Bible says, "his brothers were jealous of him" (Genesis 37:11).

Read **Genesis 37:12–26** to see what their anger and jealousy led to. Then, match the right surface sin to each blank.

Joseph's brothers __*plotted*__ to kill him. They __*grabbed*__ him and __*threw*__ him into a pit. They __*stripped*__ him of his beautiful robe. Then they __*sold*__ him as a slave to some traders. The traders took Joseph from his father's homeland to Egypt. The brothers __*lied*__ to their father and said Joseph was dead.

WORD LIST:
sold   plotted   lied   threw   grabbed   stripped

Notice how the behavior of Joseph's brothers started with anger and jealousy in their hearts. The anger and jealousy grew in them until they made some terrible, mean choices.

Now read **James 4:1–2**.

What causes fights and quarrels among you? Don't they come from your desires that battle within you? You want something but don't get it. You kill and covet, but you cannot have what you want. You quarrel and fight. (NIV)

According to this verse, where do conflicts come from?
Desires (things we want) that battle within us

Circle the words desires and want and covet in the verse. We have desires and things we covet. Our hearts WANT something. When we can't have it, we get mad. We treat others badly.

Each student below WANTS something that results in them being angry or treating others badly. Match what each student wants with what they're feeling in their heart.

"I want to be right. I can't stand being wrong! When my mom or dad corrects me, I get defensive and argue with them about it."

Pride

"I want a better life. No one likes me at school. I don't have any friends because I have so much homework. My life is awful!"

Self-pity

LIST OF HEART CONDITIONS:

Jealousy
Greed & envy
Pride
Fear of others
Selfishness
Anger
Self-pity

"I want revenge. If someone hurts me or embarrasses me, it makes me want to do something even worse to them. I won't rest until I get them back and I won't be nice to them!""

Anger

"I want my friends to approve of me. Last week my friend wanted to take something that wasn't hers. I might have helped her by telling her not to, but I was afraid she wouldn't like me if I disagreed. I'm even more afraid to tell her about Jesus. Who knows what she might think?!"

Fear of others

LIST OF HEART
CONDITIONS:

Jealousy
Greed & envy
Pride
Fear of others
Selfishness
Anger
Self-pity

TALK ABOUT IT

Are you like any of those students? What things do *you* want that lead you to treat others badly—and end up in conflict? Give an example of when that's happened.

The next part of this lesson will explain what you can do to resolve conflicts. But by now, you've been studying *What's Up?* long enough that you might have some good ideas without having to be told. So before you start part 2, think: what have you learned in past lessons that might help you fix conflict when it happens? Write down your answer and share it with the group.

OPTIONAL STOPPING POINT

If you're stopping the lesson here for today, send your students home with *something to think about* and *prayer*.

SOMETHING TO THINK ABOUT

Tell students: Pick a student (from the exercise where you identified their heart conditions) that seems most like you. This week notice how that behavior in you leads to conflict with others.

PRAYER

Use this prayer time as a period of confession. Lead your students in a very brief prayer, thanking God that he helps us in our sins and won't condemn us when we confess. Then give students several minutes to pray quietly on their own. Instruct them to:

- ★ *Confess to God their sins that create conflict.*
- ★ *Ask his forgiveness.*
- ★ *Ask his help in repenting of those sins.*

Close by thanking God for his forgiveness and fatherly care.

When you restart this lesson later, begin with *review*.

REVIEW

Ask students to tell about the conflict with his brothers that Joseph has early in his life. Remind them that conflicts with others often come because, in our hearts, we want things we cannot have.

PART 2: HOW CONFLICTS ARE RESOLVED

(About 40 minutes. Leave time for prayer and to share a personal story at the end of this part of the lesson.)

When you treat others badly, it shows you have a problem in your heart. Your surface sin comes from things you want—idols—in your heart! Do you remember what you can do about idols in your heart? (HINT: Think ocean, dorsal fin, and razor-sharp teeth.)

REVIEW

The SHARK taught you that surface sins (like treating others badly) come from idols in your heart. You learned to do two things about that:

1. You learned to <u>believe</u> all that God gives you in Jesus. Jesus is better than your idols. You've especially learned to believe that God is your loving, caring Father—so you'll act like a son or daughter.

2. You learned to <u>trust the Holy Spirit</u> by praying and spending time in God's Word. The Spirit helps you fight sin and believe.

What about the conflicts Joseph had in his life? Did *he* do those two things? Did he believe and trust God? He did!

In Egypt, Joseph trusted God and became a successful household manager. **Read Genesis 39:3.** Who was with Joseph, making him successful?

The Lord

Joseph was falsely accused of a crime and put in prison. There, he kept trusting God. **Read Genesis 39:23.** Who stayed with Joseph, making him successful?

The Lord

Finally, Joseph got a chance to interpret a dream for the Pharaoh. He was put in charge of the whole country of Egypt. He stored up food and was able to save many people from starving when a terrible famine came. **Read Genesis 41:38.** Who was Joseph's helper, working with him and in him to make him so successful?

The Spirit of God

During the famine Joseph's brothers went to Egypt to buy food. Joseph remembered how they'd harmed him. What would *he* do to *them* now that he was in charge and had the food they needed?

Well, Joseph gave them free food. He wept with joy. He told them who he was and said not to worry:

> "I am your brother Joseph, the one you sold into Egypt! And now, do not be distressed and do not be angry with yourselves for selling me here, because it was to save lives that God sent me ahead of you." (Genesis 45:4–5 NIV)

Later, his brothers asked Joseph to forgive them. He wept again and spoke to them more:

> Joseph said to them, "Don't be afraid. Am I in the place of God? You intended to harm me, but God intended it for good to accomplish what is now being done, the saving of many lives. So then, don't be afraid. I will provide for you and your children." And he reassured them and spoke kindly to them. (Genesis 50:19–21 NIV)

Check the statements you think are TRUE REASONS why Joseph could be kind to his brothers even though they'd been so mean to him.

❑ Joseph understood and believed that God had been very kind to him, so in his heart he was able to be kind to others.

❑ Joseph believed in God's saving work. This was more wonderful and important to him than what others had done to him.

❑ Joseph tried very hard to be nice even though he was angry. It worked because he was an especially nice guy.

❑ Joseph decided it was easier to forget what had happened and just pretend his brothers hadn't been so mean.

❑ Joseph believed that God had loved him and cared for him like a Father. This mattered more to him than how his brothers treated him.

❑ Joseph did everything by working together with God's Spirit, who was always with him and in him, helping him to behave like a child of God.

The first two boxes and the last two should be checked. If necessary, help your students to see that these statements are about (1) believing in the fatherly goodness of God and (2) relying on the Spirit.

TALK ABOUT IT

How did Joseph act like a son of God instead of like an orphan? (If necessary, review the lists in the last lesson that compare the thinking of orphans and sons/daughters. Pick some of the son/daughter items that fit Joseph's forgiveness of his brothers.)

Possible items from the orphan vs. son/daughter list that apply to Joseph include:

★ *"I think of others first. I don't need to put myself first because I know God will take care of me."*

★ *"God is in control of my life. He knows what's best."*

★ *"I've been mean too sometimes. But God is so good to me that when others are mean I can focus on what's good."*

★ *"I trust that God is filling my life with good things even when it's hard to see hard they're good."*

Take your time discussing how Joseph's trust in God made him able to forgive his brothers and resolve their conflict. This is the key point of this lesson.

Because of Jesus, you can be like Joseph too!

<u>Jesus saves you</u> from sin and death. That's even better than being saved from famine. Believing God's kindness to you will help you want to be kind to others.

<u>Jesus gives you</u> the Holy Spirit to always be with you and in you. You have the same power Joseph had to act like a child of your heavenly Father.

Because you're the son or daughter of such a great Father, the Bible gives you some radical instructions about how to deal with conflicts. Read what it says:

> *"You have heard that it was said, 'You shall love your neighbor and hate your enemy.' But I say to you, Love your enemies and pray for those who persecute you, so that you may be sons of your Father who is in heaven." (Matthew 5:43–45)*
>
> *Repay no one evil for evil. . . . To the contrary, "if your enemy is hungry, feed him; if he is thirsty, give him something to drink; for by so doing you will heap burning coals on his head." Do not be overcome by evil, but overcome evil with good. (Romans 12:17, 20–21)*
>
> *Let all bitterness and wrath and anger and clamor and slander be put away from you, along with all malice. Be kind to one another, tenderhearted, forgiving one another, as God in Christ forgave you. (Ephesians 4:31–32)*

Circle four things these verses say to do for your enemies and those who hurt you.

Love them. Pray for them. Feed them. Give them something to drink.

You can't overcome evil by being evil. <u>Underline</u> how a child of God *can* overcome evil.
With good

Put a star by the reason why you should forgive those who do wrong to you.
God in Christ forgave you.

It's hard to love others well—especially when there's conflict! It starts with forgiving others as God forgave you. It might also mean doing something nice for others or going to them and talking to them about the conflict. This could be SCARY. But God and the gospel help us to do it.

Sin means you get hurt and hurt others. But God is saving you from sin. His Spirit helps you love others, even when someone's been mean.

Point to remember:
When you fight sin, don't try to do it by yourself.
Do it by trusting God.

PRAY ABOUT IT

You've already trusted God by reading his Word. Now trust him more by praying. You can pray in a group or write your prayer below. Pray for three things:

1. Pray that God would <u>help you believe</u> his goodness and act like his son or daughter.

2. Pray that God would <u>make you kind</u> to people who are mean to you.

3. Pray that God would <u>make you brave</u> to talk to people you're mad at and fix conflicts.

SHARING OPPORTUNITY: Before prayer, this would be an excellent time for you to share an example from your own life of how you dealt with a conflict in a godly way. Think of a time when you had to forgive, or be kind to someone who'd hurt you, or overcome evil with good—or a time when you had initiated the conflict and had to repent of your behavior. Especially if prayer and/or remembering your status as a child of God helped you to resolve the conflict, share that story with your students now. If some of them have similar stories they want to share, allow them to do so also.

As always, treat prayer seriously and give it the time it deserves. Prayer is one key way we actively trust in God rather than ourselves. Model this trust in God by being quick to lead your students in authentic, dependent prayer, and by encouraging them to do the same.

End by looking again at these statements about conflicts. This time, circle the words that make these statements correct.

- **Conflicts start IN MY HEART / WITH SOMEONE BEING MEAN.**

- **I should treat others THE SAME WAY THEY TREAT ME / WITH LOVE.**

- **I should pray for those who are kind to me, BUT NOT / AND for those who are mean to me.**

- **I need THE HOLY SPIRIT / MORE SELF-EFFORT to help me love my enemies.**

- **I NEED / DON'T NEED to forgive others if I'm going to love them.**

- **I can overcome evil BY BEING EVIL BACK / WITH GOOD.**

- **It's OKAY / NOT OKAY for me to pretend to be nice to someone, then talk badly about them behind their backs (they deserve it anyway—they're really mean!).**

- **Loving someone means I NEVER HAVE ANY CONFLICT WITH THEM / FIX MY CONFLICTS WITH THEM.**

In my heart

With love

And

The Holy Spirit

Need

With good

Not okay

Fix my conflicts with them

MAKE IT STICK:

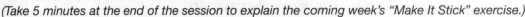

THE ORPHANS VS. SONS/DAUGHTERS FIGURE

(Take 5 minutes at the end of the session to explain the coming week's "Make It Stick" exercise.)

INSTRUCTIONS:

- ❏ Fill out this Make It Stick page during the week.
- ❏ Don't forget to bring your *Student Guide* back next time you meet.
- ❏ If you have time, go ahead and get started now.

Think of a person you struggle to get along with. This week's assignment is to pray for *that person* at least four times—yes, do it AGAIN and AGAIN and AGAIN.

When you pray, ask God to do four things:

1. Ask God to help you forgive the person for ways they've hurt you.

2. Ask God to show you some ways you can be kind to that person and love them.

3. Ask God to make you brave to do those kind things, remembering how he is kind to you.

4. Think of a specific thing that would be nice or helpful to that person, and ask God to do it for them.

To get started, take a moment right now to pray for the person. Use the Praying for Someone checklist to keep track of the rest of your praying this week.

PRAYING FOR SOMEONE

Directions: Think of a person you have trouble getting along with. You will pray for that person *four times.* Pick a time of day to do it. (If you miss your time, you can still pray later, but try to remember.)

I will pray for this person at _____ for four days.
                                              (time of day)

Now use this checklist to keep a record of your daily prayers.

DAY ONE
❑ I asked God to help me forgive the person for ways they've hurt me.
❑ I asked God to show me ways to be kind to that person.
   (If he *did* show you a way to be kind, write that way here.) _____
❑ I asked God to make me brave to do that kind thing, remembering how kind God is to me.
❑ I asked God for a specific thing he would do to be nice or helpful to that person.

The specific thing I asked God to do today was _____.

DAY TWO
❑ I asked God to help me forgive the person for ways they've hurt me.
❑ I asked God to show me ways to be kind to that person.
   (If he *did* show you a way to be kind, write that way here.) _____
❑ I asked God to make me brave to do that kind thing, remembering how kind God is to me.
❑ I asked God for a specific thing he would do to be nice or helpful to that person.

The specific thing I asked God to do today was _____.

DAY THREE
❑ I asked God to help me forgive the person for ways they've hurt me.
❑ I asked God to show me ways to be kind to that person.
   (If he *did* show you a way to be kind, write that way here.) _____
❑ I asked God to make me brave to do that kind thing, remembering how kind God is to me.
❑ I asked God for a specific thing he would do to be nice or helpful to that person.

The specific thing I asked God to do today was _____.

DAY FOUR
❑ I asked God to help me forgive the person for ways they've hurt me.
❑ I asked God to show me ways to be kind to that person.
   (If he *did* show you a way to be kind, write that way here.) _____
❑ I asked God to make me brave to do that kind thing, remembering how kind God is to me.
❑ I asked God for a specific thing he would do to be nice or helpful to that person.

The specific thing I asked God to do today was _____.

LESSON 12

I'M SO SORRY—NOT!

Big Idea: False Repentance

NOTES TO THE LEADER

This lesson has no optional stopping point and should not be divided. If you have a short class period and normally divide lessons into two sessions, you may need to work through this lesson more quickly than usual to get through it in time. If necessary, skip the third example in part 2—people of Judah and Israel. Simply skip to the conclusion at that point in the lesson and wrap things up.

LESSON GOAL

Students will learn that feeling bad about sin—and even stopping some sin—is not necessarily the same as true, godly sorrow and repentance. By seeing the selfishness of false repentance, they will start to long for deeper, true repentance.

SUMMARY

This is the first of two lessons about false and true repentance. This lesson will teach your students to recognize false repentance and see why it's less than what God requires. The next lesson will focus more on appreciating true repentance.

PART ONE of this lesson will explain that there are two ways to be sorry about sin. You can be sorry for what happened to you (that you got caught, that things turned out badly, that you feel guilty, that God might be mad), or you can be sorry for the sin itself because it displeases God. You and your students will discuss examples of "repentance" that falls short of what God wants—hating sin because you love your Father.

PART TWO will study three examples of false repentance in the Bible:

★ *King Saul's false repentance after he disobeyed God when fighting the Amalekites.*

★ *Judas's false repentance after he betrayed Jesus.*

★ *The false repentance of the people of Israel and Judah criticized by the prophet Micah in Micah 6.*

The lesson will end with prayer and encouragement that sons and daughters of God can truly repent, as he requires, in the power he gives.

YOUR PREPARATION

STUDY. Read the lesson and make sure the difference between false and true repentance is clear to you. In particular, understand that having bad feelings about past sin is NOT necessarily a sign of godly sorrow. Those bad feelings may stem from selfishness or self-pity, not from an actual hatred of sin because it displeases God. Read the three Bible passages (not just the excerpts in the lesson, but the whole passages) that are used as examples of false repentance. These are:

★ *1 Samuel 15 (King Saul)*

★ *Matthew 26:6–16; 27:3–10 (Judas)*

★ *Micah 6:1–8*

If, after reading these and the Lesson, you still aren't sure why the "repentance" they describe is false, go ahead and read Lesson 13, "I'm So Sorry—Really!" ahead of time. The examples of true repentance contained in that Lesson ought to help you see the difference. Finally, for additional reading on the topic of true and false repentance, you might consider reading Thomas Watson's The Doctrine of Repentance, which can be found in several places online. Much of the material contained in this Lesson and the next is presented more fully in Watson's essay.

BE READY TO SHARE. There's no specific sharing opportunity in this lesson but, as always, any personal stories that illustrate the lesson's points would be a great addition to you time with your students.

BEFORE YOU BEGIN

(5–10 minutes)

Talk about your assignment from last time to pray for someone you have trouble getting along with. What was good about it?

You probably noticed that the assignment included asking God to make you brave to love that person and be kind to them—but you weren't assigned to actually *do* any nice things or say something to that person. If praying did lead you to do something kind, that's great! But what did you think of an assignment to <u>pray</u> about something instead of an assignment to <u>do</u> something?

What do you think might be some good reasons for an assignment to <u>pray</u> instead of an assignment to <u>do</u>? Discuss.

There might be several good reasons:

As the following page explains, it's critical that we remember to trust God and work with him when we're trying to resolve conflict or repent of any sin. Starting with prayer is a good practice that helps us to always depend on God.

Also, starting with prayer means paying attention to our hearts, not just taking outward action. Prayer might prepare us to love the other person from the heart, not grudgingly.

Prayer gives us courage too. Time spent with our Father, through the Son, builds confidence that we're God's children and can do all things through Christ, who strengthens us. So prayer prepares us to do hard things.

TODAY'S LESSON

Sometimes you might try to do something good <u>for</u> God—but forget to do it <u>with</u> God. You forget to trust him for help. He's on your side! He works in you.

So it's good for you to be kind to the person you prayed for, but you needed to pray first. That helps you do it *with God* instead of . . .

. . . to feel proud about yourself.

OR

. . . to prove to God how good you are.

OR

. . . just so life will go better for you.

In today's lesson, you'll learn how working *with God* is important whenever you repent of sin.

PART 1: TWO WAYS TO BE SORRY

(20 minutes)

In this section, you'll learn how there's a difference between being sorry about what happened when you sinned and being truly sorry for the sin itself.

Read this story. It's a real story that happened to one of the authors of this lesson.

> *The young teacher stood on the playground. It was the second day of school and so far things had gone well. But then she noticed two of her second graders were rolling on the ground. A small crowd of students began to form around the two boys. They were fighting. She rushed over and called out for the boys to stop. They were so engrossed in punching each other, they didn't hear their teacher. Finally, she took each boy by his collar and pulled them apart. They were covered in grass and dirt with sweat running down their faces. In her anger, the teacher yelled, "You both apologize to one another right now!" Glaring at one another, both boys clenched their teeth and practically growled, " I'm sorry."*

From the story above, do you think the two boys really were sorry for hurting each other? What clues do you have that, although they stopped fighting, they didn't really repent the way God wants?

Students should be able to quickly see that the two boys weren't really sorry in their hearts, nor did they come to hate their sin. They only said they were sorry because they had to. Help your students to understand that too often we settle for this sort of fake sorrow. This lesson is about moving beyond that, to true and godly repentance.

Look up **2 Corinthians 7:10**. Fill in the blanks to see what the Bible says about two kinds of being sorry.

Godly sorrow (or grief) brings

repentance

and leads to

salvation .

But worldly sorrow brings

death .

GODLY SORROW
is being <u>Sorry for your Sin</u>.

WORLDLY SORROW
is being <u>Sorry for what happened to you</u>
because of your Sin, like . . .

- ☐ Sorry you got caught
- ☐ Sorry you feel guilty
- ☐ Sorry you had bad consequences
- ☐ Sorry you might have made God mad at you
- ☐ Sorry you don't feel good about yourself

GODLY SORROW
means you hate Sin like God does.

WORLDLY SORROW
means you still wish you could get away with
your Sin, even if you've decided to stop doing it.

These students all have ideas about repentance. Circle the ones you think are right ideas about the kind of being sorry God wants. Then tell why you think they're right—or not.

"I cheated on a test and got caught. It turned out very badly for me. Boy, am I sorry I ever cheated. I've learned my lesson. No more cheating for me! I've repented."

"I lied to my mom. She didn't catch me, but now I feel SO guilty about it. I need to make sure I never do that again. It's feels horrible! I've repented."

"I'm going to start obeying my parents better. They need to see that I've changed. If I can have fewer fights with them, life will go easier for me. I need to repent."

"I like to say unkind things about people. But I know it makes God unhappy with me. So last time, after I gossiped about my classmate, I went home and was extra nice to my sister. I want to show God that I can be nice too. He'll see. I'm repenting."

TALK ABOUT IT

False repentance is VERY common. Give some more examples you can think of.

As you discuss, help students to see that, although feeling sorry is a part of true repentance, feeling guilty doesn't necessarily mean they've repented God's way. It could still be a worldly, selfish sort of sorrow. Godly sorrow comes to hate sin and be disgusted with it—not for selfish reasons, but because it disgusts God: "You will remember your past sins and despise yourselves for all the detestable things you did" (Ezekiel 36:31 NLT).

PART 2: IDENTIFYING FALSE REPENTANCE

(55 minutes: If you have a short class session and usually divide the lessons, you will probably have to skip the third example—people of Israel and Judah—in order to finish on time. If time is tight when you get to that point, simply skip down to the conclusion to read 1 John 3:9–10 and close your class time with prayer.

Now see if you can tell what's wrong in some examples of false repentance in the Bible.

NOT real repentance example:
King Saul

God told King Saul to fight the evil Amalekites and kill all the people and their animals. Saul fought them, but decided to keep some alive. God's prophet Samuel went to scold Saul for disobeying God.

Saul made excuses. He said, "I did *most* of what God told me. It was the people—not me—who didn't want to follow God's instructions. We only kept some animals so we could offer them as sacrifices to God."

But Samuel saw that Saul's heart was against obeying God. He said God wouldn't let Saul keep being king. Samuel also refused to honor Saul by travelling home with him. When Saul saw that his excuses weren't working, he decided to say he was sorry. Read what he said:

> *"I have sinned. I violated the LORD's command and your instructions. I was afraid of the people and so I gave in to them. . . . But please honor me before the elders of my people and before Israel; come back with me." (1 Samuel 15:24, 30 NIV)*

<u>Underline</u> the words Saul said that sound like repentance.

Now think of at least three ways you can tell Saul wasn't really sorry for his sin even though he said some good-sounding things.

1. _____

2. _____

3. _____

Good answers might be:

- ★ *He only said he was sorry after his excuses didn't work.*
- ★ *He was still thinking about himself. He was mostly worried he'd look bad to the elders if Samuel didn't come with him.*
- ★ *He just said he was sorry so Samuel and God wouldn't be mad at him anymore.*
- ★ *He's still partly blaming other people and repeating his excuses.*
- ★ *His first reaction when confronted with his sin was to make excuses, not to repent. He was hoping to get away with his sin, not turn from his sin.*
- ★ *Saul doesn't seem brokenhearted over his sin, just worried about having been caught.*

TALK ABOUT IT

Give an example of a sin someone your age might be caught doing. In that situation, how might you be tempted to make excuses or say you're sorry just to avoid bad consequences instead of repenting in your heart? Share your example with the group, or write the false repentance words you might say.

Encourage students to come up with several real-life examples. Take the time to have them express or write out, in their own words, the sort of things they say that look sorry even when they aren't sorry in their hearts for the sin itself.

NOT real repentance example:
Judas

Judas was one of Jesus's disciples. He did a horrible thing. He betrayed Jesus by telling people who wanted to kill him how best to arrest him. He got paid thirty pieces of silver for it. Jesus was arrested, put on trial, and killed.

After the trial, Judas felt guilty. He was so sorry about what happened that he tried to give the silver pieces back to Jesus's enemies. Read what happened:

> Then when Judas, his betrayer, saw that Jesus was condemned, he changed his mind and brought back the thirty pieces of silver to the chief priests and the elders, saying, "I have sinned by betraying innocent blood." They said, "What is that to us? See to it yourself." And throwing down the pieces of silver into the temple, he departed, and he went and hanged himself. (Matthew 27:3–5)

Underline the parts of the passage that show how Judas felt guilty and sorry about the way his evil plan turned out.

But which kind of sorrow did Judas have?

_____ A godly sorrow that leads to salvation

_____ A worldly sorrow that brings death

Judas never repented of being greedy for money and hating Jesus in his heart. He was just trying to get rid of his guilty feelings. What things did he do that show he was only trying to make himself feel better?

Judas confessed his sin and tried to give back the money. When that didn't work, the only way to stop feeling guilty was for him to kill himself. Students may feel that Judas appeared truly sorry, but help them to see that feeling guilty is not the same thing as being truly sorry for the sin itself.

TALK ABOUT IT

Give an example of a sin someone your age might do and then feel guilty about. In that situation, what things might you do instead of repenting in your heart—just to feel less guilty?

Give students time to come up with several examples. Having them express what they do to feel less guilty after they sin will help them understand false repentance. You may want to point out that faith in Jesus is the only way any of us are actually not guilty. Jesus covers our guilt so that we can repent sincerely—out of love for God and hatred of sin—without any need to prove ourselves righteous.

NOT real repentance example:
People of Judah and Israel

You may have to skip this example if time is tight.

The leaders and shopkeepers in the countries of Judah and Israel were enjoying good times. They were getting rich. But they were doing it by cheating the poor people and taking land that wasn't theirs. They also worshiped idols.

They knew they were sinning, but they thought they could get away with it if they also did some things for God, like give him offerings.

God sent his prophet Micah to say this to them:

> *What can we bring to the LORD?*
> > *What kind of offerings should we give him?*
> *Should we bow before God*
> > *with offerings of yearling calves?*
> *Should we offer him thousands of rams*
> > *and ten thousand rivers of olive oil?*
> *Should we sacrifice our firstborn children*
> > *to pay for our sins?*
>
> *No, O people, the LORD has told you what is good,*
> > *and this is what he requires of you:*
> *To do what is right, to love mercy,*
> > *and to walk humbly with your God. (Micah 6:6–8 NLT)*

Underline the things the people offered to do for God to make up for their sin. Then circle the kind of repentance God really required.

Now think of at least three ways (more if you can) that the people's wrong repentance was different from the right repentance God required. Share your answers with the group and talk about them.

1. _____

2. _____

3. _____

The things those people offered to do for God sound WAY too extreme, don't they? Isn't it amazing how they would rather do *anything else* than truly repent in their hearts?

Sin is like that. It can make you think you would rather do *anything else* than repent in your heart. That's why you do wrong repentance instead.

CONCLUSION

Godly repentance is HARD. You'll never do it without God's help. You need to work with God to repent.

Read 1 John 3:9–10. Fill in what it says about sons and daughters of the Father:

"No one born of God makes a practice of

sinning_____, for God's seed abides in him, and he cannot keep on

sinning_____ because he has been

born of God_____. By this it is evident who are the

children_____ of God."

PRAY ABOUT IT

Finish by praying that God would make that verse true in your life. Pray as a group or write out your prayer below.

1. Thank God that his Spirit is in you, helping you to repent.

2. Pray that you would deeply believe that you are a child of your loving Father.

3. Pray that you would stop wrong repentance and be able to repent in your heart.

MAKE IT STICK:

HOW I RESPOND TO CORRECTION

(Take 5 minutes at the end of the session to explain the coming week's "Make It Stick" exercise.)

INSTRUCTIONS:

- ☐ Fill out this Make It Stick page during the week.
- ☐ Don't forget to bring your *Student Guide* back next time you meet.
- ☐ If you have time, go ahead and get started now.

Godly repentance honors God and brings deep joy. You'll learn more about it next time. Spend the coming week noticing how you usually respond when your parents or someone else (like a teacher) correct you. Godly repentance is the best response, but be honest. If you do something else, it's good to notice that so you can confess it to God and work on it with his help.

HERE'S YOUR ASSIGNMENT:

1. Notice a few times in the coming week when you are corrected.

2. On the "How I Respond to Correction" table, write down what you did that needed correction.

3. Then check how you responded when you were corrected.

4. Be prepared to discuss your results next time.

WHOOPS! MY BAD.

How Do I Respond to Correction?

I WAS CORRECTED ABOUT:

_____

_____

_____

I RESPONDED BY:

HIDING MY SIN

- ❑ "I didn't do that."
- ❑ "You misunderstood me."
- ❑ "It looked worse than it really was."
- ❑ "You're being unfair!"

MAKING EXCUSES

- ❑ "Someone else started it."
- ❑ "I couldn't help it. I was tired, hungry, angry…"
- ❑ "I did good things too. Doesn't that count?"
- ❑ "You did something wrong too."

FALSE REPENTING

- ❑ "I'll change because I have no choice."
- ❑ "I'll change to show you I can be good."
- ❑ "I'll change so I won't feel guilty anymore."
- ❑ "I'll change … but no more than I have to."
- ❑ "I'm sorry it turned out this way for me."
- ❑ "I'm sorry you feel the way you do."

TRUE REPENTING

- ❑ "I'm sorry in my heart for my sin."

I WAS CORRECTED ABOUT:

_____

_____

_____

I RESPONDED BY:

HIDING MY SIN

- ❑ "I didn't do that."
- ❑ "You misunderstood me."
- ❑ "It looked worse than it really was."
- ❑ "You're being unfair!"

MAKING EXCUSES

- ❑ "Someone else started it."
- ❑ "I couldn't help it. I was tired, hungry, angry…"
- ❑ "I did good things too. Doesn't that count?"
- ❑ "You did something wrong too."

FALSE REPENTING

- ❑ "I'll change because I have no choice."
- ❑ "I'll change to show you I can be good."
- ❑ "I'll change so I won't feel guilty anymore."
- ❑ "I'll change … but no more than I have to."
- ❑ "I'm sorry it turned out this way for me."
- ❑ "I'm sorry you feel the way you do."

TRUE REPENTING

- ❑ "I'm sorry in my heart for my sin."

I WAS CORRECTED ABOUT:

_____

_____

_____

I RESPONDED BY:

HIDING MY SIN

- ❑ "I didn't do that."
- ❑ "You misunderstood me."
- ❑ "It looked worse than it really was."
- ❑ "You're being unfair!"

MAKING EXCUSES

- ❑ "Someone else started it."
- ❑ "I couldn't help it. I was tired, hungry, angry…"
- ❑ "I did good things too. Doesn't that count?"
- ❑ "You did something wrong too."

FALSE REPENTING

- ❑ "I'll change because I have no choice."
- ❑ "I'll change to show you I can be good."
- ❑ "I'll change so I won't feel guilty anymore."
- ❑ "I'll change … but no more than I have to."
- ❑ "I'm sorry it turned out this way for me."
- ❑ "I'm sorry you feel the way you do."

TRUE REPENTING

- ❑ "I'm sorry in my heart for my sin."

LESSON 13

I'M SO SORRY—REALLY!
Big Idea: Godly Repentance

LESSON GOAL

Students will understand the nature of true repentance and will come to appreciate it, want it for their lives, and work at it.

SUMMARY

The last lesson looked at false repentance. This one will turn your students' attention toward true repentance. Although true repentance can be difficult and often looks daunting, this lesson ought to be approached with expectation and joy. It's about the amazing change of heart children of God are called to and enabled to live out.

PART ONE will look at examples of true repentance in the Bible, much as the last lesson looked at examples of false repentance. You and your students will examine (1) David's repentance following his sin with Bathsheba, and (2) the repentance of the prodigal son in Jesus's parable. These passages display several critical elements of true repentance, including:

★ *A contrite heart*

★ *Sorrow over having offended God*

★ *Sincere confession*

★ *Godly shame*

★ *Hatred for the sin*

★ *A turning away from selfishness and back to God*

PART TWO is about the many reasons God's people have to embrace true repentance joyfully. Your students will take a close look at the kindness of God toward sinners who repent, and will be urged to pray for repentance and practice it. It's so worth it, even though it seems so hard.

YOUR PREPARATION

*STUDY. Reread the parable of the prodigal son from **Luke 15:11–32** (which you studied for Lesson 6). Also read the account of David's sin with Bathsheba in **2 Samuel 11 and 12**, along with his prayer of repentance in **Psalm 51**. As you read, let your heart sense the ugliness of sin and the sweetness of repentance. Although sin is a shameful thing for God's people, repentance is always a noble act that ought to encourage us. God loves to see us repent!*

BE READY TO SHARE. Prepare to tell your students a story about true repentance in your life, preferably one that show how you're growing and learning to repent in ways you used to not do. You'll have an opportunity to share your story at the end of part one.

PRAY. Most people don't like to admit their sin or to admit that they need to keep repenting again and again. As a result, repentance feels distasteful and holds little joy. But that feeling is so wrong! Pray that your students would be able to see that godly repentance is a noble and sweet activity for God's children—one unlike any other! Pray that they and you would come away from this lesson eager to repent, believing it will bring joy.

BEFORE YOU BEGIN

(10 minutes)

Share your results from the "How I Respond to Correction" chart. How did people try to correct you this week? How did you catch yourself responding to them?

> *Use this sharing time in part as an opportunity to review the characteristics of false repentance. In particular, be sure students remember that it isn't godly sorrow merely to be sorry for sin's consequences or results, nor to want guilty feelings gone, nor to give up some sins merely for selfish reasons or prideful performance.*

What did you learn about your habits? Do you usually use being corrected as an opportunity to repent? Or have you gotten used to certain ways of avoiding repentance or practicing false repentance?

> *Help students see their need for more godly repentance in their lives. Seeing our bad patterns shouldn't make us feel guilty if we're joined to Jesus and know his forgiveness, but it ought to make us eager for something better.*

TODAY'S LESSON

Now that you're aware of false repentance, it's time to learn about more about godly repentance. First, you'll learn what it looks like. Then you'll learn what makes it so sweet.

To get started, check the statements you think sound like godly repentance. Then turn the page to begin.

_____ You **see** and admit the sin in your heart, not just the surface sins you do, with no excuses.

_____ You're **sorry** for your sin because it's horrible to God, not just because it turned out badly for you.

_____ You have a broken heart that's **sad** and ashamed at how you treated your heavenly Father.

_____ You **stop** doing *all* kinds of sin you see, not just a few sins you don't mind giving up.

PART 1: GODLY REPENTANCE— WHAT IS IT?

(35 minutes)

If you checked ALL of those statements, you're right. All of them are part of godly repentance. Let's look at an example of godly repentance in the Bible.

Real repentance example:
King David

Kind David wanted the wife of one of his most loyal soldiers, Uriah. So he brought her to his palace and behaved with her like she was his wife. Then to hide that sin, David got rid of Uriah. He ordered that Uriah be put in a dangerous place in battle and abandoned there—to be killed. Once Uriah was dead, David married his wife.

Those were terrible sins and David had bad consequences from them. But God helped him to see how horrible they were, and David repented. He wrote about his repentance in Psalm 51. Read some of the things he said in his prayer to God:

> For I know my transgressions,
>   and my sin is always before me.
> Against you, you only, have I sinned
>   and done what is evil in your sight,
> so that you are proved right when you speak
>   and justified when you judge.
> Create in me a pure heart, O God,
>   and renew a steadfast spirit within me.
> The sacrifices of God are a broken spirit;
>   a broken and contrite heart,
>   O God, you will not despise. (Psalm 51:3–4, 10, 17 NIV)

Underline some parts that show David was concerned with his heart, not just surface sins.

Circle a part that shows David wasn't making any excuses.

Put a star next to a part that shows David was sorry because his sin was horrible to God, not just for the consequences.

Put a sad face next to a part that shows David had a broken heart that was sad and ashamed.

Put a smiley face next to a part that shows David was willing to turn and live for God with his whole heart.

Real repentance example:
The Younger Son

Jesus taught about godly repentance, too, in his parable of the two sons that you studied in Lesson 6. In Jesus's story, the younger son asked his father for the family money he'd get when the father died. Then he left home and wasted the money in wild living. When it was gone, he was hungry and had to feed pigs. Read the rest of the story.

When he came to his senses, he said, "How many of my father's hired servants have food to spare, and here I am starving to death! I will set out and go back to my father and say to him: Father, I have sinned against heaven and against you. I am no longer worthy to be called your son; make me like one of your hired servants." So he got up and went to his father.

But while he was still a long way off, his father saw him and was filled with compassion for him; he ran to his son, threw his arms around him and kissed him.

The son said to him, "Father, I have sinned against heaven and against you. I am no longer worthy to be called your son."

But the father said to his servants, "Quick! Bring the best robe and put it on him. Put a ring on his finger and sandals on his feet. Bring the fattened calf and kill it. Let's have a feast and celebrate. For this son of mine was dead and is alive again; he was lost and is found." So they began to celebrate. (Luke 15:17–24 NIV)

Underline the parts that show the son was sorry because his sin was horrible to his father and to God, not because of the consequences to himself.

"I have sinned against heaven and against you."

Put a squiggly line under the parts that show the son was heartbroken and ashamed by his sin and no longer proud or demanding.

"I am no longer worthy to be called your son; make me like one of your hired servants."

Is the son repenting for what he'll get out of it, or is his selfishness gone? How can you tell?

Help students to see that although the son realizes his life will be better off if he repents and goes back to the father, he doesn't do this with a selfish agenda but rather with a humble one. He has given up living for whatever he thinks will bring him happiness and is humbly submitting to the father's plan for his life, whatever that is—like a servant would. Repentance does bring us a better life than remaining in sin. We can recognize this and yet not repent in a scheming, what's-in-it-for me way.

Now draw a picture of what you think the son looked like when he repented to his father. What does his face look like? What's he doing with the rest of his body? Draw your picture below.

 There are many good ways to imagine the repentant son, based on the story. Encourage students to think about godly repentance and express it creatively here.

Explain to the rest of the group what you put in your picture of the son. What about it shows godly repentance?

OPTIONAL STOPPING POINT

If you're stopping the lesson here for today, send your students home with *something to think about* and *prayer*.

SOMETHING TO THINK ABOUT

Tell students: look back at the true repentance checklist under TODAY'S LESSON at the beginning of this lesson. Notice how each item in the list has a key word that starts with "s":

★ *You SEE and admit your sin.*

★ *You're SORRY for your sin.*

★ *You're SAD and ashamed over your sin.*

★ *You STOP all kinds of sin.*

Use those "s" words to remember what true repentance is like and to think about your repentance.

PRAYER

Pray together that you and your students would enjoy full, true repentance.

★ *Have four students volunteer to pray aloud for the group, each taking one of the elements on the checklist above and asking God to grant that kind of repentance.*

★ *Thank God that he's always delighted to hear from his children who repent.*

When you restart this lesson later, begin with *review*.

REVIEW

Remind the students of the story of the two stories that highlighted true repentance: (1) David's repentance following his sin with Bathsheba, and (2) the repentance of the prodigal son in Jesus's parable. Let them tell you about the characters and what happened. Also review these elements of true repentance:

★ *SEE – A contrite heart that admits sin with no excuses*

★ *SORRY – Sorrow over having offended God*

★ *SAD – Godly sadness and shame over sin*

★ *STOP – A turning away from all kinds of sin (not just a few you pick) and back to God*

Imagine you could read the thoughts of students when they have an opportunity to repent. Some would be NOT SORRY. Others would be REALLY SORRY. Here are some students and the two ways each might think.

NOT SORRY

REALLY SORRY

"I don't sin as much as others, so I don't have to apologize for anything."

"There's sin in my heart and it often shows up in how I act. I have much to be sorry for."

"When I get corrected, my first thought is to blame someone else or say it isn't true."

"When I get corrected, I'm eager to examine my heart and see my sin so I can repent."

NOT SORRY   # REALLY SORRY

TALK ABOUT IT

Which NOT SORRY and REALLY SORRY ways of thinking sound the most like your own life? Circle three places that sound like ways you tend to be NOT SORRY, or that sound like ways you're becoming more REALLY SORRY. Give an example from your life that fits something you circled.

The figure ought to provide plenty of opportunities for students to see how they fail to measure up to God's standard in repentance. Try to also help them see the positive side of this: that the "really sorry" side of the figure describes an incredibly humble and attractive person—and they can be that person. Help them gain a sense of longing for the sort of repentance that's possible for saved-in-Christ people.

SHARING OPPORTUNITY: Pick a pair of thoughts from your life and give an example. Try to make it not just an example of how you fail or succeed in being really sorry, but an example of progress and growth in your life—how you've improved as you've gotten to know and appreciate Jesus better.

PART 2: GODLY REPENTANCE— WHY DO IT?

(35 minutes)

Does godly repentance seem too hard? Well, you have to do it while *working with God*. Jesus said to remain in him: "Apart from me you can do nothing" (John 15:5).

Start by remembering how much your Father loves you because of Jesus. When you confess your sin to him, he won't scold you. He *loves* to welcome you. He's eager to help you.

When you come to him to repent, God acts toward you like the father in Jesus's story acted toward the younger son. So go back a few pages to that story. Put a big smiley face by every place you can find that shows how much the father loves the son—even though that son has been sinning.

 Make sure students take some time to focus on the father in the story by adding those smiley faces.

Now, like you drew a picture of the son, draw a picture of how you think the father looked while the son was confessing and repenting. What does *his* face look like? What's *he* doing with his body? Draw your picture below.

Show your picture to the group. Tell what you put in your picture that fits how God welcomes you when you come to him in repentance.

Good pictures might show the father's joy, his eagerness to welcome the son, his compassion, his delight in honoring the son, his spirit of forgiveness or his love for the son. The father is delighted and celebrates as fully and grandly as possible. This is God's heart toward repentant sinners.

JUST THINK . . .

❏ Sin is the most hideous evil and the filthiest thing about you—and you're getting rid of it!

❏ You're coming closer to your Father who loves you!

❏ You're serving Jesus! There's no one and nothing better.

❏ When you repent you're like the younger son, greeted with honor and celebration and a humungous hug. There's joy in heaven!

❏ Your sin is shameful, but repenting has *nothing* to be ashamed about. It's God-honoring and noble—the *very best* thing you could do today!

❏ God is *so* kind to you that you're joined to Jesus, forgiven, and allowed to repent!

ARE YOU THINKING, DIDN'T I DO THIS?

Does this lesson seem a lot like Lesson 6, when you imagined what the father was thinking and wrote it out? That's on purpose! It's because remembering God's love for you, a sinner, is something you need to keep doing— again and again. Never forget how Jesus died for you and God welcomes you as an eager Father—or else you'll never cry over your sin or want to repent.

Godly repentance is SWEET! There's sadness involved, and much struggling. But the end result is great joy.

PRAY ABOUT IT

Pray now with your group. Do three things when you pray:

1. Thank God. Pick some of the great things about repentance mentioned above that make you most eager to repent. <u>Underline</u> the ones you picked, and then thank God for them. You can also pick something about your picture of the Father and thank God for that.

2. Ask God to make your heart eager to repent. Pray with confidence in the Holy Spirit. He's on your side and lives in you to do exactly what you're asking!

3. Ask God to bless you with repentance. You might need to pray about specific sins you know you need to repent of. Ask God to help you give them up and turn to him. (If the sins you need to repent of aren't appropriate to share with the group, you can pray this part silently or write out your prayer.)

Leave plenty of time for prayer. There's a lot to pray about here, and it's probably best to break up your prayer time into three sections. Let students read the first point and do that prayer, then stop and do the second, then stop again before doing the third.

MAKE IT STICK:

KEEP PRAYING FOR REPENTANCE

(Take 5 minutes at the end of the session to explain the coming week's "Make It Stick" exercise.)

INSTRUCTIONS:

❑ Fill out this Make It Stick page during the week.

❑ Don't forget to bring your *Student Guide* back next time you meet.

❑ If you have time, go ahead and get started now.

Look back at the examples from your life that you circled in the list of NOT SORRY and REALLY SORRY ways to think about repentance. Write the REALLY SORRY side of those examples here.

1. _____

2. _____

3. _____

This week when you pray, ask God to:

❑ Make you more REALLY SORRY in the ways you wrote down.

❑ Help you to notice when you're NOT SORRY and when you're REALLY SORRY.

Put a check mark by each REALLY SORRY way of thinking every time you pray about it this week.

LESSON 14

I (GULP) FORGIVE YOU

Big Idea: Forgiving Others

NOTES TO THE LEADER

LESSON GOAL

Students will grow in their appreciation of what it means to be forgiven by God, and will see how this results in a heart that's eager to forgive others.

SUMMARY

This lesson will continue applying the gospel's work in the heart to the relationships your students have with others. The topic this time is forgiveness. Your students will learn how God's people forgive because they've been forgiven.

PART ONE will explain why believers forgive, using Jesus's parable of the unforgiving servant who'd been forgiven a great debt but refused to forgive a small one owed to him. That parable will also be retold in two comic-book stories about current-day students who experience forgiveness. The second of those stories will make a direct connection between a student knowing she's forgiven by Jesus and finding the desire to forgive others. You'll have much opportunity for discussion with your students about forgiveness.

PART TWO will focus on how much we ought to forgive, calling attention to how much God has forgiven us and to Jesus's instruction to forgive seventy times seven. Your students will learn that forgiveness is costly to the one who forgives. They will learn the difference between true (costly) forgiveness and false forgiveness, and you and they will discuss how to forgive fully.

YOUR PREPARATION

STUDY. Read the lesson and the comic-book stories carefully and understand the main point they're making about forgiveness—that those who've been forgiven ought to forgive others. Also study the passage from Jesus's teaching on forgiveness that's used in this lesson, **Matthew 18:21–35**.

BE READY TO SHARE. The topic of forgiveness should provide good opportunities to tell about your own experiences. In particular, be ready to add to the discussion at the end of the lesson by telling about a time when God helped you to truly forgive another person. You'll have to be able to explain what it cost you to forgive that person and how your forgiveness was demonstrated in your actions towards them. Make it clear that although forgiveness begins in the heart, it shows itself in actions.

PRAY. This lesson will make little impact with your students (except maybe to make them feel guilty) unless they delight in God's forgiveness of them. So pray that they, and you, would know and appreciate forgiveness in the days leading up to the lesson.

BEFORE YOU BEGIN

(10 minutes)

Talk about last time's assignment to pray that you'd notice when you're NOT SORRY and when you're REALLY SORRY. What did you notice about how you usually think? Share an example of a time when you noticed yourself behaving in one of those ways.

Help students to remember the difference between false and godly repentance and to be able to apply it to actual situations in their lives. Urge them to share specific examples if they can.

Sometimes people get so used to NOT SORRY thinking that it gets very hard to be REALLY SORRY. Do you think that's happened with you? Did you remember to pray to God and keep asking him to bless you with true repentance?

Be sure not to scold students for admitting to NOT SORRY thinking. Urge them to keep turning to God, especially if they become discouraged with their struggles to truly repent. Assure them that such struggles continue all our lives and ought only to cause them to rely even more on God. He is eager to help them.

TODAY'S LESSON

Remember that you'll never *want* to repent and obey God unless you know HOW MUCH he's already forgiven you. In this lesson, you'll learn how your heavenly Father's forgiveness also makes you able to forgive others.

First you'll learn *why* you ought to forgive. Then you'll learn *how much* you ought to forgive.

PART 1: WHY SHOULD I FORGIVE?

(About 35 minutes)

Read the story, *The Board that Soared*.

Ethan loved his skateboard. His family was poor, but Ethan had saved enough money to buy the board. He rode it everywhere—that is, everywhere except down the walkway to the neighbor Mrs. Vincent's driveway and flower garden. Mrs. Vincent was poor too. Ethan knew she barely had enough money to put gas in her old car, drive to the store, and buy groceries for herself and seeds for her much-loved garden. His dad had warned him many times never to ride his skateboard down the walkway. "You might lose control and land in Mrs. Vincent's flowers—or worse," he told him.

One day Ethan decided he just HAD to try the walkway on his board.

> I can make it! Besides, who cares about those stupid flowers anyway?

Whoops!

The board flew right into the windshield of Mrs. Vincent's car!

The windshield would have to be replaced. It'd cost hundreds of dollars.

His dad told him they didn't have the money to pay for the damage and that Ethan would have to work every Saturday until he could pay Mrs. Vincent for a new windshield. He even suggested that Ethan sell his skateboard in order to pay her back!

It's okay, Ethan. I guess I'll walk to the store until I can save enough money for a new windshield. You don't have to pay me anything.

I'm so sorry, Mrs. Vincent. I know I can't pay you, but please don't make me work or sell my skateboard!

Ethan was so grateful that he couldn't stop thanking Mrs. Vincent for her kindness.

The next day Ethan came home from school to find his sister Sarah riding his skateboard.

As he watched, it slipped from under her and landed on a rock. The skateboard got badly scratched.

I'm so sorry! I should have been more careful. Will you forgive me?

What might Ethan say? Fill in how you think he might respond to his sister.

Students can either write what they think is the best or "right" answer, or what they think would be an expected answer in that situation. There are no wrong answers.

TALK ABOUT IT

Share with the group what you wrote for Ethan to say. Also tell what you think he *should* say.

Do you think Ethan's experience the day before with Mrs. Vincent should make him MORE LIKELY or LESS LIKELY to forgive his sister? Why?

Students should be able to see that Ethan would be MORE LIKELY to forgive his sister after being forgiven by Mrs. Vincent. He knows what it feels like to have done something that'll cost him greatly and then to be forgiven. He's still feeling relieved, and it should make him merciful.

The story about Ethan is like a story Jesus told. Read Jesus's story in **Matthew 18:23–35**.

Why was the master right to be so angry with the servant who wouldn't forgive? Discuss.

In both stories, someone was **forgiven**.

Forgiveness:
Not counting what someone owes you, or how they hurt you,
against them anymore even though they still deserve it.

Think about that. Forgiveness makes little sense. Why would you decide to not count what someone owed you or how they hurt you—*unless you'd been forgiven too?!*

Jesus told his story to make you think of how God has forgiven you. If you realize how being forgiven by God is THE VERY BEST THING that's ever happened in your life, then you'll want to forgive others too. Then it makes sense.

Point to remember:
When you treasure how God forgives you, you'll also forgive others.

The Bible says being forgiven by God means you forgive others.
Fill in the blanks to complete these verses.

Colossians 3:13. As the Lord has forgiven you, so you also must *forgive*_____.

Mark 11:25. Whenever you stand praying, forgive, if you have anything against anyone, so that your *Father*_____ also who is in heaven may forgive you.

Now look at those two verses. The first one says that you should forgive because God forgave you. But the second one says something a bit different. Tell how it's different.

The Bible says forgiving others is part of being forgiven by God. They go together so much that if you don't forgive, you shouldn't think God is really forgiving you. If you really know how big a sinner you are and how much God forgives you, it *will* make you forgive others.

You don't have to be forgiven for a skateboard mishap to have a reason to forgive others. Children of God *always* have a reason. Read another story, *The Unkind Friend,* to see how this works.

The Unkind Friend

Katie arrived at school and started looking around for her friends. There was one—Amber! She was talking and laughing with some of the more popular girls.

Katie walked up.
Amber hadn't noticed her yet.

Really, Katie is such a loser. I don't know why I act like she's my friend.

Oh—Katie. Um . . . I didn't see you.

Wh . . . What did you say?

> Come on girls, let's go. We don't have to talk to this loser.

Katie and Amber didn't speak the rest of the day. Katie was hurt . . . and mad! She started thinking of ways she could make *everyone* hate Amber. A few times when she looked at Amber, Amber looked the other way. Katie thought her used-to-be friend might have been feeling guilty, but not really sorry.

"ONE WEEK LATER"

A week went by. Katie wished she could heal her conflict with Amber. She knew it meant she had to forgive Amber—even though Amber didn't deserve it and hadn't even asked! So Katie prayed.

> Father, help me to stop counting Amber's mean words against her. Help me to stop hating her for what she did.

Katie also knew she had said mean things herself sometimes. God had forgiven her for those words—and much more. Katie thanked God that he forgave her for *so much*. He forgave her for *every* sin she'd *ever* done!

> Thank you, Father, for forgiving me so completely.

The next day Katie saw Amber at school. She knew she might never be able to fully trust Amber again. But she still wanted to heal their conflict and start wishing good things for Amber.

⭐ What might Katie say? Fill in what you think she might tell Amber.

There's no right answer here. Students might write something that shows forgiveness or they might think Katie wouldn't (or shouldn't) forgive Amber yet. Both kinds of answers are fine—it's whatever the student thinks might happen.

TALK ABOUT IT

Share what you wrote for Katie to say. Do you think the way Katie knew and treasured God's forgiveness should make her MORE LIKELY or LESS LIKELY to be able to forgive Amber?

Again, students should be able to see that Katie would be MORE LIKELY to forgive Amber because she treasures how God forgives her. (NOTE: They don't necessarily have to believe that Katie should forgive Amber, or that Amber has displayed suitable repentance—but they should be able to see that forgiveness is more likely because Katie knows God's forgiveness.) Help students to see that we don't need to have an experience like Ethan had in order to want to forgive others. We should always be ready to be forgiving, because we always have the biggest and best forgiveness of all—God's forgiveness.

Like Katie, you need to truly treasure the forgiveness you've received from God and know how BIG it is. It's much bigger than the forgiveness Ethan got from Mrs. Vincent. It lets you forgive even very hurtful sins like what Amber did to Katie.

OPTIONAL STOPPING POINT

If you're stopping the lesson here for today, send your students home with *something to think about* and *prayer*.

SOMETHING TO THINK ABOUT

Tell students: This week ask yourself how often you pray the way Katie did in the story when she thanked God for how much he'd forgiven her. Especially if you hardly ever (or never!) thank God for his forgiveness, try to remember to do that several times this week. Without being thankful to God for how he forgives you, you'll have a hard time forgiving others. Forgiving others lets us acknowledge their sin but still be kind to them—just like Jesus has done for us.

PRAYER

Make your closing prayer together like Katie's prayer in the story.

- ★ *Thank God for his forgiveness and kindness to you and your students in spite of all your sin.*

- ★ *Ask God to help you see how much you're forgiven and to use that to help you forgive those who hurt you.*

Remind your students to keep praying this way during the week.

When you restart this lesson later, begin with *review*.

REVIEW

Remind students of Jesus's parable of the unforgiving servant who'd been forgiven a great debt but refused to forgive a small one owed to them. Let them also tell you about the story of Ethan and the skateboard. Make sure they include details about each character and what happened.

PART 2: HOW MUCH SHOULD I FORGIVE?

(40 minutes)

If *your* forgiveness is based on God's forgiveness of you, that helps you know how much you should forgive others. Fill in the blanks to tell how big God's forgiveness is, looking up Bible verses to help.

God forgives me OF EVERYTHING. He cleanses me from
<u>all unrighteousness</u> (1 John 1:9).

God forgives me COMPLETELY, AS MUCH AS HE CAN. He removes my sins from me as far as
<u>the east is from the west</u> (Psalm 103:12).

God forgives me WITHOUT KEEPING A RECORD OF HOW BAD I WAS. He
<u>cancels the record of debt that stood against us</u>, nailing it to the cross (Colossians 2:14).

Forgiveness is always costly to the person who forgives.

When the master in Jesus's story forgave his servant, it cost him much money.

- - - - - - - - - - - -

When Mrs. Vincent forgave Ethan, it cost her being able to use her car to go to the store.

- - - - - - - - - - - -

When Katie forgave Amber, it cost her the chance to get even for how she'd been hurt.

God forgives me WITH THE MOST COSTLY PAYMENT OF ALL. Jesus ransomed me (bought me back) not with silver or gold, but with

_his blood_____ (1 Peter 1:18–19).

Just like there's false repentance, there can be FAKE FORGIVENESS. It usually involves saying, "I'll only forgive you if . . ." It means you still want the other person to pay somehow instead of accepting the cost of forgiveness yourself.

Look at some of the ways Katie might have "forgiven" Amber.

FAKE FORGIVENESS #1:

"I'll forgive you this one time. But you better not say mean things about me again."

FAKE FORGIVENESS #2:

"I'll only forgive you if you're really sorry. That's for your own good, you know."

FAKE FORGIVENESS #3:

"If you do something for me to make up for what you did, then maybe I'll forgive you. Otherwise I'd just be letting you get away with being mean."

FAKE FORGIVENESS #4:

"I forgive you. But you should know I'm only doing it because I'm a Christian and I have to."

Now match each kind of fake forgiveness with how Katie still wanted Amber to pay. Put the number from the fake forgiveness above next to the attitude below that fits it.

__2__ "You have to pay by feeling bad."

__4__ "You have to pay by knowing I'm still mad at you."

__3__ "You have to pay by paying me back."

__1__ "You have to pay by never sinning against me again."

TALK ABOUT IT

Do any of these kinds of fake forgiveness sometimes seem right to you? Which ones? Why? Discuss how they might just be ways to make the other person pay?

Encourage students to honestly discuss their reservations about forgiveness. Sometimes forgiveness feels unjust, so it may seem unfair to forgive. And it's true that looking for some restitution or repentance from the other person is often an important part of loving them and fully healing the relationship. But forgiveness means a change from wanting the person who wronged you to suffer to wanting good for that person. We can forgive freely, bearing the cost of forgiveness, and still care for the other person in ways that help them repent or make restitution— if doing so is a way to love them. Forgiveness means we're truly concerned with loving the other person. Fake forgiveness may use the guise of loving them, but really wants them to pay.

It's easy to think of reasons to limit your forgiveness. The disciple Peter once asked Jesus, "Lord, how often should I forgive someone who sins against me? Seven times?" (Matthew 18:21 NLT). Peter wanted to put a reasonable limit on how much he had to forgive.

"No, not seven times," Jesus replied, "but seventy times seven!" (v. 22 NLT).

Can you do that math? 70 x 7 =
___490___ times.

Wow! That's a lot of forgiveness. Jesus says to keep forgiving again and again. Based on what you've learned about forgiveness, check why you think you should not limit how much you forgive.

_____ Because God wants to test you by commanding something really hard.

_____ Because Christians are supposed to let people take advantage of them.

_____ Because God forgives you for the same horrible thing again and again, with no limits.

The last answer is the best one. By now, students should be able to see that our forgiveness of others—including how we forgive—flows from God's forgiveness of us. Peter foolishly thought seven times would be a lot of forgiveness. This showed he had little sense of how horribly he himself had sinned against God time after time, and yet had been forgiven. A person slow to forgive others often has little sense of the horror of his own sin.

TALK ABOUT IT

End by talking about a time when someone did wrong to you. Share what happened, or write it or draw a picture of it below. (If you prefer, you can imagine how someone *might* do wrong to you.)

You may have to give students suggestions or examples of the kinds of ways others have done wrong to them. Has someone said something mean to you? Have they taken something that was yours? Have they told lies about you? Hurt you?

How could you show true forgiveness to that person because Jesus forgave you?
Consider these questions:

❑   What would it cost you to forgive them?

❑   How could you show that you don't count what they did against them anymore?

Discuss your answers with the group, and pray that God would help you to forgive.

Lead students through the essence of repentance—bearing the cost of the wrong and not counting the sin against the other person. It's always good to remind students of God's forgiveness toward them, and to pray if forgiveness seems difficult.

SHARING OPPORTUNITY: Here you too can tell a story of a time when God helped you to truly forgive another person. Be sure to include (1) what it cost you to forgive and (2) how you show that you don't count what that person did against them anymore.

MAKE IT STICK:

PICK A FAVORITE THING YOU'VE LEARNED

(Take 5 minutes at the end of the session to explain the coming week's "Make It Stick" exercise.)

INSTRUCTIONS:

❑ Fill out this Make It Stick page during the week.
❑ Don't forget to bring your *Student Guide* back next time you meet.
❑ If you have time, go ahead and get started now.

There's just one more lesson left. Before the last lesson, think back through all the lessons and pick something that really impressed you. Do you have a favorite part?

(HINT: If you can, you might want to look back though your lessons or your Make It Stick pages to remind yourself of what you've done. Otherwise, just see what you can remember.)

Once you pick something, write it in the space below or draw a picture that makes you think of it. Be ready to tell what was the BEST THING you learned.

LESSON 15

LET'S. KEEP. GOING.

Big Idea: A Lifetime of Faith

NOTES TO THE LEADER

LESSON GOAL

Students will recall many of the important lessons they've learned during this course, and will consider how to apply them as they continue a life of faith.

SUMMARY

This lesson will prepare your students to continue living by faith by reminding them of some of the key principles they've learned in this course and by teaching them to keep using them. Believing the gospel is not just a one-time event that marks the start of the Christian life. It's also an ongoing practice that's essential for growth. A figure that accompanies this lesson imagines life as a journey that can be lived either in unbelief or in belief. The traveler approaches four "cities":

★ *"Idolopolis" — where unbelief means you live for idols, but belief means you live for God*

★ *"Orphantown" — where unbelief means you depend on yourself, but belief means you depend on God*

★ *"Repentance City" — where unbelief means false repentance, but belief means godly repentance*

★ *"Crossville" — where unbelief means you make excuses for sin, but belief means you admit sin and trust Jesus*

PART ONE will introduce the "journey" and give you and your students a chance to discuss what they've learned and how they've grown—and how they hope to grow still more.

PART TWO will use Abraham's test of faith, when he was told to sacrifice his son Isaac, as an example of how the lessons learned in each "city" help us to live by faith and obey God.

Your students will see how Abraham passed the test because he overcame potential idols, resisted orphan thinking, truly repented, and trusted the cross.

PART THREE will reinforce an idea central to all those "cities"—that a believer's identity comes from being joined to Jesus; clothed in him. Your students are prone to think their identity comes from what others think of them. They tend to feel ashamed or proud based on those opinions of others. In this final part of the lesson, they need to be reminded that who they are is based on Jesus. When they believe this, what others think can't make them ashamed or proud anymore.

SUPPLEMENTAL FIGURE

You'll use the Journey of Faith Figure (Fig. 15-1) in part 1 of this lesson.

YOUR PREPARATION

STUDY. Read the lesson and, if necessary, go back and re-study the lessons it reviews:

★ *Lessons 8 and 9 about idols and looking under the surface (the shark)*

★ *Lesson 10 about orphans and sons/ daughters*

★ *Lessons 12 and 13 about true and false repentance*

★ *Lesson 7 about big repentance and big love (the Cross Figure)*

*Also read the entire account of Abraham's test of faith, found in **Genesis 22**. You should be aware, too, that the idea of being clothed in Christ comes not only from Galatians 3:27, which is mentioned in the lesson, but also from Romans 13:14 (NIV)—where it's a command: "Clothe yourselves with the Lord Jesus Christ, and do not think about how to gratify the desires of the flesh."*

BEFORE YOU BEGIN

(10 minutes. If this lesson is presented in two parts, do this section at the beginning of the second part of the lesson.)

Share the best thing you've learned so far from *What's Up?* Can you see any change in your life from what you've learned? Give an example.

Pray together. Thank God for what each person has learned and how they've grown in Jesus. Ask him to keep working in you.

TODAY'S LESSON

This lesson will look back at much of what you've already learned and review it. It'll also look ahead at how you can *use* what you've learned for the rest of your life. Think of it as a road trip. There are places you've been and places you're going. We'll call it "the journey of faith."

PART 1: YOUR JOURNEY

(15 minutes)

Much of what you've learned in *What's Up?* could be summed up by **Galatians 2:20**. Look up that verse and fill in the blank to complete the statement below.

I live
<u>by faith</u>   in the Son of God, who loved me and gave himself for me.

Your life is a <u>journey of faith</u>. Faith means believing in Jesus and trusting him. You need to . . .

- ❑ Believe God's promises
- ❑ Believe God loves and accepts you (because you're joined to Jesus)
- ❑ Believe God forgives you (because of Jesus)
- ❑ Believe God welcomes you as his child (because of Jesus)
- ❑ Believe you're holy in Jesus and becoming even more holy

TALK ABOUT IT

Look at the Journey of Faith figure. Imagine the road trip represents the rest of your life. Along the way, you'll have many choices. You can choose to "drive" with *unbelief* or with *belief*.

Talk about the "cities" along the way. Each stands for a way of *unbelief* or *belief*. Which do you think you've learned the most about? Where have you grown in faith? Where do you most still need to grow?

Point to remember:
You don't have to try hard to have extra strong faith. What matters is that your faith is in an extra strong person—Jesus!

IMPORTANT NOTE: If your students are prone to try to grow by self-effort, they may hear that growth is by faith and start to think, "Now I must try really hard to have strong faith." Explain to them that faith isn't like that. Rather, it's about resting in Jesus and receiving help from him. Even faith itself is a gift from God (Eph. 2:8). This is why we pray during What's Up? lessons and why you will pray again with your students at the end of this lesson. Faith is received from God, not mustered up by trying harder to believe better.

	WELCOME TO IDOLOPOLIS	**WELCOME TO ORPHANTOWN**	**WELCOME TO REPENTANCE CITY**	**WELCOME TO CROSSVILLE**
Unbelief When I am full of doubt . . .	**My idols control me.** They're like the shark (Lesson 9).	**I depend on myself** like the orphan in Lesson 10.	**My repentance is false.** I'm sorry for what happened to me (Lesson 12).	**I make excuses for my sin.** I don't think about Jesus much (Lesson 7).
Belief When I have faith in Jesus. . .	**God is in charge of my life.** The shark is being killed.	**I depend on my Father** like a son or daughter.	**My repentance is godly.** I am sorry for sinning against God (Lesson 13).	**I admit my sin and trust Jesus for forgiveness.** My trust in Jesus and love for him grows.

Give students a chance to look at the figure and recall the lessons it summarizes. Help them see how belief is the necessary foundation for each of the godly behaviors they've learned about.

- ★ *Without first believing, they will love idols more than God.*
- ★ *Without first believing, they won't trust God to be a loving Father.*
- ★ *Without first believing, they can't be truly sorry for sin but will instead wish they could get away with it.*
- ★ *Without first believing, they won't have the confidence to admit their sin and let the cross grow large in their lives.*

PART 2: ABRAHAM, MAN OF FAITH

(30 minutes)

Now let's look at how the journey of faith worked in the life of Abraham. Of course, Abraham never studied *What's Up?*, but the Bible shows us that he learned all those lessons.

REVIEW

Several lessons ago, you studied a time when Abraham (he was called Abram at the time) failed to live by faith. Remember when he went to Egypt . . .

Abraham didn't believe God would bless him like he promised.

SO . . .

Abraham gave in to the idol of fear that he might be killed.

SO . . .

Abraham lied about his wife, Sarah.

Later in Abraham's life, his faith grew stronger. God also gave him a son, Isaac. That started to fulfill one of the big promises God had made—that through Isaac, Abraham would have many descendants (great-great-grandchildren). Isaac gave Abraham and Sarah much joy!

But read what happened when Isaac was partly grown:

After these things God tested Abraham and said to him, "Abraham!" And he said, "Here I am." He said, "Take your son, your only son Isaac, whom you love, and go to the land of Moriah, and offer him there as a burnt offering on one of the mountains of which I shall tell you." (Genesis 22:1–2)

DIRECTIONS:

Find the word "tested" and circle it. God was testing Abraham's faith. It would take faith for Abraham to do what God said.

Also find the words "burnt offering" and circle them. A burnt offering was a sacrifice to pay for sin. God told Abraham to kill Isaac to pay for sin. What a horrible price to pay!

When God told Abraham to sacrifice Isaac, what idols do you think Abraham might have had in his life that tempted him not to obey that command? Think of a few (you don't have to fill in all the blanks).

What might Abraham have LOVED more than he loved God?

_____

_____

_____

_____

What might Abraham have TRUSTED more than he trusted God?

_____

_____

_____

_____

What might Abraham have FEARED that came before God?

_____

_____

Abraham might have loved (more than he loved God):

Isaac, the joy of being a father, seeing God's promises playing out

He might have trusted:

Isaac, having the promises come true the way he'd always imagined

He might have feared:

Losing Isaac, the sadness of having to kill his son, the uncertainty of being without a son again

To pass the test, Abraham had to believe God would still keep his promises, make him happy and completely bless him—even if Isaac were killed. In fact, Abraham did believe something huge about God. **Read Hebrews 11:17–19** to see what Abraham believed.

Abraham believed that God was able to

raise Isaac from the dead _____.

WELCOME TO ORPHANTOWN

Abraham also had to <u>believe</u> that God loved him and was taking care of him like a Father. For each pair below . . .

❑ Cross out the orphan thinking that would have led Abraham to disobey God.

❑ (Circle) the thinking like a son that Abraham needed in order to obey God.

Finally, decide which example of orphan thinking would have been most tempting.

"I just CAN'T fail with Isaac. It's up to me to make sure nothing bad happens to him."

"It's okay for me to be weak and trust God. He has a good plan even if something happens to Isaac."

"Isaac finally made me into a person who's worth something— a father! I'll be worthless again without him."

"My worth as a person comes from belonging to God. Not even losing Isaac can take that away from me."

"I've been trying hard to obey God and he should have noticed how good I've been. It isn't fair that he's making me do this!"

"God counts me righteous because I believe, not because of how good I can be. He always gives me more than I deserve."

"Even if I don't have Isaac, I still have so very much love from God."

"If I don't have Isaac, I've lost everything!"

The left column is orphan thinking for the first three items. The right column is orphan thinking for the last item. Help students to see how Abraham had to believe in God's goodness and loving care.

To obey God, Abraham must have repented. For example, maybe he was tempted to love Isaac more than he loved God, and he'd had to work on repenting of that.

Think of some of the excuses and false obedience (obeying with a selfish attitude) Abraham could have tried. Put a star by the ones that sound like something you'd be tempted to try.

"I'm not sure I understood you right, God, so I'm going to hold off on this. See, I'm trying to be obedient. I don't want to make a mistake with something so important."

"What you said isn't fair, God. I deserve better. You need to consider that."

"Okay, I'll do it. But how soon do I have to start? Do I have to do it NOW?"

"If I do this, I hope you don't expect me to like you anymore—because I won't."

"I guess I have to do this because you're God, and if I don't you can make my life terrible. So I will."

Abraham didn't try any of these. Instead, the Bible says he saddled his donkey early the next morning and left with Isaac to sacrifice him at Moriah. Along the way he said good things about God's care, not bad things. Discuss what you think Abraham must have <u>believed</u> in order to have such true obedience and repentance.

Help students to see that Abraham obeyed not just by taking the minimum necessary actions, but with his heart. He must have believed in God's goodness even when God's command seemed like a bad thing in his life.

WELCOME TO
CROSSVILLE

Finally, Abraham had to <u>believe</u> that he was a big sinner, but God would find a way to pay for his sin. Abraham lived many years before Jesus. He didn't know about the cross. But he still believed that God himself would be the one to pay for sin.

God had said Isaac would be the burnt offering. But Abraham believed God actually had a better plan. Read what happened as he and Isaac climbed the mountain at Moriah, and <u>underline</u> what Abraham said God would do.

Isaac said to his father Abraham, "My father!" And he said, "Here I am, my son." He said, "Behold, the fire and the wood, but where is the lamb for a burnt offering?" Abraham said, "God will provide for himself the lamb for a burnt offering, my son." (Genesis 22:7–8)

Sure enough, after Abraham passed the faith test and was ready to sacrifice Isaac, God called to him to stop. He provided a ram instead. Abraham and Isaac sacrificed it and worshiped God.

Years later, God provided the only sacrifice that really paid for all of Abraham's sin and for the sin of everyone else who has faith. Jesus died on the cross. He's the sacrifice that pays for your sin—ALL OF IT, no matter how bad you've been!

Circle the statement that best fits Abraham's approach to his sin.

EXCUSES: "God, most of my sin was stuff I couldn't help. It isn't fair that you ask me to sacrifice Isaac for it."

PRETENDING: "I don't sin that much. I'm really pretty good. Let me show you that the payment you demand is too steep."

ADMITTING (AND FAITH): "Yes, I'm a horrible sinner. I deserve to pay a horrible price for my sin. But I'm trusting that you will pay that horrible price instead."

Which way of thinking will make Abraham love God more? Which will make him obey better? Discuss why.

Admitting sin and living by faith clearly produces more love for God. And only love leads to the kind of robust, faith-filled obedience Abraham displayed. Excuses and pretending are only concerned with doing just enough to avoid bad consequences.

PART 3: WHO YOU ARE

(about 30 minutes)

If you have a short class session, you may have to skip this section.

★ *If you have less than 25 minutes left, skip ahead to the point in the lesson marked CONCLUSION.*

★ *If you have less than 10 minutes left, skip ahead to PRAY ABOUT IT.*

The lessons you've studied are about WHO YOU ARE if you believe. You're a person joined to Jesus, who died on the cross and rose to life for you. It makes you a son or daughter of God, because you're joined to *the* Son of God. Read what the Bible says about that:

> *You are all sons of God through faith in Christ Jesus, for all of you who were baptized into*
>
> *Christ have clothed yourselves with Christ. (Galatians 3:26–27 NIV)*

<u>UNDERLINE</u> the part that connects faith in Jesus with being a son.

<u>DOUBLE UNDERLINE</u> the part that says it's like wearing Jesus as your clothes.

That's a strange picture, isn't it—"clothed with Christ"? Try to draw that picture. In the space below, draw yourself wearing a long, white robe. Make sure the robe in your picture covers all your other clothes.

Now write "JESUS" on the robe. That's your picture of you being clothed with Christ.

THINK ABOUT CLOTHES.

You'd be ASHAMED if you were wearing no clothes. You might also feel embarrassed if you were wearing really cheap or ugly or dorky clothes.

And you might feel PROUD and better than others if you were wearing really expensive or pretty or extra cool clothes.

Well, it's easy to feel the same about what others think of you. You might be ASHAMED and try to cover up what's wrong with you if others:

❑ Think you're stupid.

❑ Catch you doing something wrong.

❑ Find out you're really pretty uncool.

❑ Notice a mistake you made.

❑ See your sin.

❑ Scold you or make fun of you.

(Put an X by one or two that might make you feel especially ashamed.)

Or you might feel PROUD and better than others if people:

❑ Think you're smart.

❑ Notice you doing something right.

❑ Never catch you making mistakes.

❑ See your good behavior.

❑ Praise you and reward you.

(Put a ★ STAR by some that make you feel proud and better than others.)

But if you're clothed in Jesus, all those things are like the clothes underneath your big robe. Who cares? They don't matter; Jesus matters instead.

Jesus forgives what's wrong with you. Jesus also gives you a righteousness that's better than anything that's right with you. Those other things can't make you ashamed or proud any more. What people think of you doesn't make who you are. _A person who's in Jesus_ is who you are!

TALK ABOUT IT

Discuss the things you put an X or a star ★ by. How would they stop mattering to you if you believed more fully that you're a son or daughter, clothed in Jesus?

You may have to walk students through the answer, or get them started with some examples from your own life, like: "I wouldn't mind so much when people saw my sin if I believed more deeply that Jesus covers that sin." "I wouldn't crave praise from people so much if I believed more deeply that God thinks the world of me due to Jesus." "I wouldn't care so much when people think I'm a nobody if I believed more deeply that, in Jesus, God treasures me with all his heart."

CONCLUSION

Now turn all the way back to Lesson 1 where you picked a word or short phrase that best fit the way you thought about Christianity when you began *What's Up?*. Copy what you wrote here:

"Christianity is _____."

Has your thinking changed because of what you've studied since then? If it has, pick a new word now to describe how you think now:

"Now Christianity seems to me to be all about _____."

Share the word you picked. Discuss what you learned that made it change.

This is another opportunity for students to share how they've grown. There's no right answer, although students will have learned well if they choose a word like "gospel" (the point of the first lesson) or "faith/belief" or "Jesus." Those are all words that take the emphasis away from what they must do for Christ and put it on Christ and his work.

PRAY ABOUT IT

God can help *you* live by faith, just like Abraham did. Use Philippians 1:6 as the theme for your closing prayer. It says:

> *"I am sure of this, that he who began a good work in you will bring it to completion at the day of Jesus Christ."*

Pray that God would keep up the good work he's begun in you. Ask him to teach you more of his great love for you and help you to believe it more deeply.

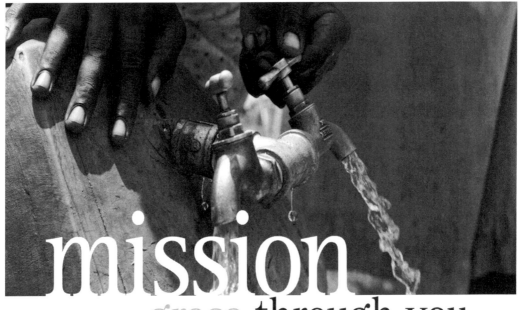

mission
grace through you

At Serge we believe that mission begins through the gospel of Jesus Christ bringing God's grace into the lives of believers. It also sustains us and empowers us to go into different cultures bringing the good news of forgiveness of sins and new life to those whom God is calling to himself.

As a cross-denominational, reformed, sending agency with 200 missionaries on over 25 teams in 5 continents, we are always looking for people who are ready to take the next step in sharing Christ, through:

- **Short-term Teams:** One to two-week trips oriented around serving overseas ministries while equipping the local church for mission

- **Internships:** Eight-week to nine-month opportunities to learn about missions through serving with our overseas ministry teams

- **Apprenticeships:** Intensive 12–24 month training and ministry opportunities for those discerning their call to cross-cultural ministry

- **Career:** One- to five-year appointments designed to nurture you for a lifetime of ministry

Serge Grace at the Fray   Visit us online at: www.serge.org/mission

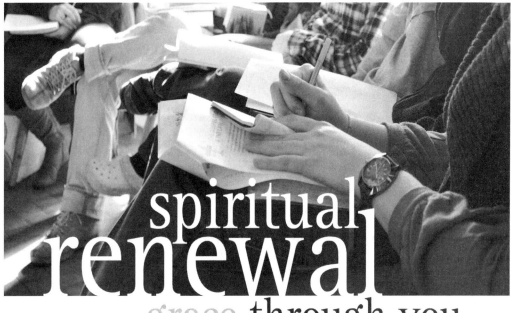

spiritual renewal
grace through you

Disciples who are motivated and empowered by grace to reach out to a broken world are handmade, not mass-produced. Serge intentionally grows disciples through curriculum, discipleship experiences, and training programs.

Curriculum for Every Stage of Growth

Serge offers grace-based, gospel-centered studies for every stage of the Christian journey. Every level of our materials focuses on essential aspects of how the Spirit transforms and motivates us through the gospel of Jesus Christ.

- 101: The Gospel-Centered Series
  (The Gospel-Centered Life, The Gospel-Centered Community)

- 201: The Gospel Transformation Series
  (Gospel Identity, Gospel Growth, Gospel Love)

- 301: The Sonship Course and Serge Individual Mentoring

Gospel Renewal for You

For over 25 years Serge has been discipling ministry leaders around the world through our Sonship course to help them experience the freedom and joy of having the gospel transform every part of their lives. A personal discipler will help you apply what you are learning to the daily struggles and situations you face, as well as, modeling what a gospel-centered faith looks and feels like.

Training to Help You Disciple Better

Serge's discipler training programs have been refined through our work with thousands of people worldwide to help you gain the biblical understanding and practical wisdom you need to disciple others so they experience substantive, lasting growth in their lives. Available for onsite training or via distance learning, our training programs are ideal for ministry leaders, small group leaders or those seeking to grow in their ability to disciple effectively.

Grace at the Fray   Visit us online at www.serge.org/mentoring

www.newgrowthpress.com

curriculum for
every stage of
growth
grace through you

Every day around the world, Serge teams help people develop and deepen the living, breathing, growing relationship with Jesus that the gospel promises. We help people connect with God in ways that are genuinely grace-motivated and that increase their desire and ability to reach out to others. No matter where you are along the way, we have a series that is right for you.

101: The *Gospel-Centered* Series

Our *Gospel-Centered* series is simple, deep, and transformative. Each *Gospel-Centered* lesson features an easy-to-read article and provides challenging discussion questions and application questions. Best of all, no outside preparation on the part of the participants is needed! They are perfect for small groups, those who are seeking to develop "gospel DNA" in their organizations and leaders, and contexts where people are still wrestling with what it means to follow Jesus.

201: The *Gospel Transformation* Series

Our *Gospel Transformation* studies take the themes introduced in our 101 level materials and expand and deepen them. Designed for those seeking to grow through directly studying Scripture and working through rich exercises and discussion questions, each *Gospel Transformation* lesson helps participants grow in the way they understand and experience God's grace. Ideal for small groups, individuals who are ready for more, and one-on-one mentoring, *Gospel Identity, Gospel Growth,* and *Gospel Love* provide substantive material, in easy-to-use, manageable sized studies.

The *Sonship* Course and Individual Mentoring from Serge

Developed for use with our own missionaries and used for over 25 years with thousands of Christian leaders in every corner of the world, Sonship sets the standard for whole-person, life transformation through the gospel. Designed to be used with a mentor, or in groups ready for a high investment with each other and deep transformation, each lesson focuses on the type of "inductive heart study" that brings about change from the inside out.

 Grace at the Fray   Visit us online at www.serge.org/resources

www.newgrowthpress.com